BLACK MANHATTAN

JAMES WELDON JOHNSON

BLACK
MANHATTAN

with a foreword by Zadie Smith

NEW YORK, NY

Printed in the United States of America.
10 9 8 7 6 5 4 3 2 1

Ig Publishing
Box 2547
New York, NY 10163
www.igpub.com

ISBN 978-163246-11-55

TO

JOHN B. NAIL

Who himself has witnessed the
past threescore years and more of
the changes herein recorded and
has been the friend of many of
the outstanding characters that
appear in these pages.

CONTENTS

FOREWORD

THE BOOK YOU HAVE IN your hands is a curio. A slice of American history composed in the midst and turmoil of that history, and yet written in a tone of determined brightness, with steady optimism . . . *Black Manhattan* must have read oddly even to its first readers: its publication coincided with the Depression. The utopian Harlem of the Roaring Twenties, so joyfully depicted by Johnson—"the principle streets never deserted, gay crowds skipping from one place of amusement to another, lines of taxicabs and limousines standing under the sparkling lights of the entrances to the famous night clubs"—was more or less out of date as soon as the ink was dry. And those who came to the book later, in 1945, or 1968, or as I did, in the early noughties, could not help but register a melancholy distance between Johnson's optimistic predictions and the complex reality of what followed. But the distance is the point. I always find reading the book a useful corrective to the current habit of overlaying the present on the past, of demanding from our ancestors the same attitudes, arguments and aims we hold ourselves.

The object of *Black Manhattan*, in Johnson's own words, was to prove that the "Negro" was a "creator as well as a creature"—an aim made only more poignant by the fact that its necessity has long passed.

But Johnson was born only eleven years after the Dred Scott Decision of 1857 (the law that established the "Negro" a non-citizen, being "so far inferior, that they had no rights which the white man was bound to respect") and his generation of Victorian black scholars and race cheerleaders took to heart the duty of proving the opposite case, as if a certain amount of black doctors or black jockeys or black chorus girls or black public school teachers would secure equal citizenship on the basis of merit proved. Race cheerleading of this kind had a very particular psychology and set of received ideas. Whereas today "appropriation" is often viewed as cultural theft, for Johnson's generation, to be worthy of appropriation signaled you had something worth appropriating, and therefore was a matter of pride:

> [The Negro's] sacred music: the Spirituals; his secular music: the plantation songs, rag-time blues, jazz, and the work songs; his folk-lore: the Uncle Remus stories and other plantation tales; and his dances. All of these have gone into and, more or less, permeated our national life. Some of them, various forms of his secular music and his dances, have been completely taken over; they are no longer racial, they are wholly national. Even the Uncle Remus stories have been appropriated and appear, with slight adaptations, in the daily newspapers as popular bedtime stories.

Even examples we consider now in a wholly egregious light, were—if are to believe Johnson—experienced differently at the time, at least by some ("Negro programs are now so popular that there are quite a number of white broadcasters who are doing Negro 'stuff.' The great favorites among these at present are Amos and Andy, whose imitations are so good that they are extremely popular with coloured people.") And though Johnson is rarely blind to painful caricature in the otherwise forgotten Broadway shows he preserves for posterity here, for him the fact that an African-American had reached a career on the stage at all was what really counted. Throughout, there is an empathetic understanding of limited choices: he doesn't judge harshly those actors who found themselves in demeaning or stereotypical roles—which was, in the final analysis, almost all of them. Instead, he registers their efforts, notes their popularity, and moves forward, to the next promising example of "progress." His even tone will frustrate many readers, but there doesn't seem much need for rhetorical inflation when the realities presented are so stark. Instead of micro-aggressions, his was the era of aggression-aggressions:

> [Jack] Johnson has said that not only did he have to fight Jeffries, but that psychologically he also had to fight the majority of the thousands of spectators, many of whom were howling and praying for Jeffries to "kill the nigger."

Sometimes, though, you wish he would notice that a critic like Mary Martin, writing for *The Nation*—and quoted at length by Johnson—only appreciates the genius of the great tap dancer Bill Robinson if she can first establish that whatever genius a "Negro" might possess must be "primal" and "unconscious" ("For Bill Robinson does not know intellectually that the capacity for rhythmic coordination is the fundament, not only of art but all human achievement . . .") or that the great nineteenth-century British actress Mrs. Kendal perhaps does not offer the great Shakespearean actor Ira Aldridge the finest compliment when she writes: "Although a genuine black, he was quite *preux chevalier* in his manners to women." But in Johnson's historical reality, this kind of sentimental paternalism was, relatively speaking, the *good* press. He collects plenty examples of the bad:

> A good part of the press and some literary fellows were industrious in formenting the sentiment that the security of white civilization and white supremacy depended on the defeat of Jack Johnson. One of these writers [. . .] wrote in the red-blooded style of the day that Jeffries was bound to win because, while he had Runnymede and Agincourt behind him, the Negro had nothing but the jungle; that the Negro would be licked the moment the white man looked him in the eye. This psychic manifestation of white superiority did not materialize . . .

It's worth noting, too, that in his genteel way, Johnson anticipates some of the arguments of the present, understanding, for example, that the unique nineteenth-century success of black men in boxing and horse racing was not the result of some innate physical gift for punching and riding but the direct consequence of what we might now call a "structural" issue: "He never gets so fair a chance in those form of sport or athletics where he must be a member of a team as in those where he may stand upon his own ability as an individual. The difficulty starts with prejudice against his becoming a team member." To say nothing of the prejudice—or legal bar—against him entering a university, the front of a train carriage, or most of the professions.

Black Manhattan is an uneven book, not in quality but in the weight it lends to its different narrative strands. At first it appears to be a piece of broad social history, outdated by the standards of modern scholarship but still fascinating; it then morphs into an account of the legal, civic, and criminal attacks on the concept of black citizenship from the mid-1600s to 1930—but somewhere in the middle it disappears into a granularly detailed account of Broadway history, emerging only a few pages before the end to consider Harlem's other great cultural legacies, literature and radical politics. But in all these disjointed sections there are things to treasure. It is wonderful to know the names of four of the eleven men who made up the original black population of Manhattan: Paul d'Angola, Simon Congo, Anthony Portugese, and John Francisco. It is always heartening to remember the greatest presidential bid ever floated: Victoria C. Woodhull for President with Frederick Douglass as her Vice, on the Equal Rights Party ticket. There are certainly more thorough accounts to be read on the history of slavery, emancipation, Reconstruction— and its subsequent dismantling—the development of Jim Crow, the scourge of lynching and the bloody racial massacres of the early twentieth century, but few provide Johnson's intense subjectivity and almost transcendent, willed belief in the possibility that every bloody setback, every unpicking of the rights supposedly guaranteed in the constitution, could be overcome with committed resistance. Dutifully he records slave rebellions, legal challenges, successful cultural milestones, and so many individual acts of resilience and defiance. Even false dawns—like Marcus Garvey's shakedown of Harlem pocketbooks, or Booker Washington's depressing political accommodations—are never wholly condemned, only quietly mourned.

Sometimes you do get a hint of something like despair. I hear it particularly in Johnson's recounting of a shameful order—issued during the First World War, by American authorities—for the instruction of

French officers in their dealings with African-American troops:

> "We must not eat with them, must not shake hands or seek
> to talk or meet with them outside of the requirements of the
> military service [. . .] We must not commend too highly
> the black American troops, particularly in the presence of
> (White) Americans. It is all right to recognize their good
> qualities and their services, but only in moderate terms,
> strictly in keeping with the truth." Out of such an order the
> great taboo could not be left: "Make a point of keeping the
> native cantonment population from 'spoiling' the Negroes.
> (White) Americans become greatly incensed at any public
> expression of intimacy between white women and black
> men." All these "don'ts" had a familiar, homelike ring.

Home was the place where you had no home, or none that could
be considered brave or free. Home was a racialized system so obsessively
applied, so totalizing, that even in wartime it had to be exported
wholesale! What is most extraordinary about *Black Manhattan*, to the
reader of today, is how much rage and despair must have had to be
swallowed to write it at all.

Johnson, alongside his fellow black Victorian, Frederick Douglass,
walked a long, tough, but ultimately hopeful road, and yet died before
much of what he hoped for came to pass. His paragraph-long obituary
for Douglass, who died in 1895—as the dream of Reconstruction died
and Jim Crow rose from its ashes—is one of the few moments Johnson
allows for the possibility that the arc of the moral universe rarely bends
towards justice in one man's lifetime:

Douglass died, probably, a disappointed man. He had lived to see many of the highest hopes for his race fall to the ground. He was a philosopher, but there were many things he saw come to pass that he hardly could have accepted with resignation. He had seen the Negro disenfranchised and all the guarantees of equal citizenship fought for and laid down for him in the fundamental law of the land flouted. He had seen the race made the victim of new hatreds and brutalities not equaled under some phases of slavery. He had the knowledge that in the ten years before his death more than two thousand of his fellows had been lynched and tortured and burnt at the stake.

Johnson died in 1938. The road of progress and disappointment, progress and disappointment, continued. Continues.

Zadie Smith, 2020

PREFACE

IT HAS NOT BEEN MY intention to make this book in any strict sense
a history. I have attempted only to etch in the background of the
Negro in latter-day New York, to give a cut-back in projecting a picture
of Negro Harlem; I have avoided statistical data and included only as
much documentation as seemed to me necessary for my main purpose;
and I have refrained from repeating expansively matter already easily
accessible in published form.

The story here related sometimes runs much beyond the
boundaries of Manhattan, but only when I have felt that the main
threads of interest led out from New York or from without back to it.

Since the text of the book was put in print, the announced
production of *Othello* with Paul Robeson in the title role—referred
to on page 179—has taken place; he opened in London at the Savoy
Theatre May 19, 1930, with triumphant success. Also, the record held
for forty-six years by Isaac Murphy—referred to on page 66—was on
May 17, 1930, equalled by Earl Sande.

I wish here to make acknowledgment to MISS RICHETTA G.
RANDOLPH for her valuable assistance in the gathering and sifting of
historical data; to MR. WILLIAM H. FOSTER and MR. IRVING JONES for
furnishing and corroborating from their intimate knowledge many

of the facts regarding the era of professional sports and of Bohemian life in the eighties and nineties and the middle period of theatrical development. I wish also to acknowledge my indebtedness for source material to THE ARTHUR A. SCHOMBURG COLLECTION.

To the JULIUS ROSENWALD FUND and its president, MR. EDWIN R. EMBREE, I wish to express my especial thanks for the grant of the Fellowship which has made possible the writing of the book.

J.W.J.
New York City, 1930

BLACK MANHATTAN

ONE

T HE FACT THAT WITHIN NEW YORK, the greatest city of
the New World, there is found the greatest single community
anywhere of people descended from age-old Africa appears at a
thoughtless glance to be the climax of the incongruous. Harlem is
today the Negro metropolis and as such is everywhere known. In the
history of New York the name Harlem has changed from Dutch to Irish
to Jewish to Negro; but it is through this last change that it has gained
its most widespread fame. Throughout coloured America, Harlem is
the recognized Negro capital. Indeed, it is Mecca for the sight-seer,
the pleasure-seeker, the curious, the adventurous, the enterprising,
the ambitious, and the talented of the entire Negro world; for the lure
of it has reached down to every island of the Carib Sea and penetrated
even into Africa. It is almost as well known to the white world, for it
has been much talked and written about.

So here we have Harlem—not merely a colony or a community
or a settlement—not at all a "quarter" or a slum or a fringe—but a
black city, located in the heart of white Manhattan, and containing
more Negroes to the square mile than any other spot on earth. It
strikes the uninformed observer as a phenomenon, a miracle straight
out of the skies.

But the seeming incongruity and wonder of this black metropolis in the heart of the great Western white metropolis grows less and less and disappears as we glance backward from Harlem and become familiar with the story of the Negro in the City and State of New York. The anomaly of the situation starts to fade out the moment we take account of how far back the story begins.

Henry Hudson, under the flag of the Dutch East India Company, sailed up the Hudson River in 1609; the Dutch West India Company was established in 1614; and New Netherland was founded as a Dutch colony in 1623. Governor Peter Minuit bought Manhattan Island from the Indians and established the settlement of New Amsterdam—New York City—in 1626. Within the same year there were eleven Negroes in the colony, constituting a little above five per cent of the total non-Indian population. There is a record of the names of four of these eleven Negroes: Paul d'Angola, Simon Congo, Anthony Portuguese, and John Francisco. These names appear to have some bearing on the origins of the men who bore them, and they also carry a suggestion of romance. What was the history of these first Negroes landed on Manhattan? There is nothing to tell the tale. The eleven were all men, and the probabilities are that they were captured seamen, for the Dutch West India Company was actually a naval power and waged war upon the high seas. These Negroes were landed at New Amsterdam and made bondservants; but there were instances at a later date when Dutch commanders, not knowing what to do with them, let captured blacks go free. Two years later three Negro women were landed at New Amsterdam.

Under a system of patroonship the number of Negroes in the colony increased, but only slowly; and it was not until a definite system of slavery was established that it grew rapidly. Slavery was never quite profitable in New Netherland under the Dutch; so it never actually flourished. But the Dutch surrendered to the English in 1664; and under the English, who had found slave labour profitable in Virginia, slavery became an institution in New York. Thirty years after the English occupation of the colony there were 2,170 Negroes in New York, a little more than thirteen per cent of the whole colonial population. Under English rule the trade in black human beings was extended and became lucrative. The laying out of plantations in Westchester County and on Long Island and Staten Island was an important factor in the development of the trade. The settling of whites and blacks on the land in these three sections began at the same time. In 1709 a slave-market was established at the foot of Wall Street.

Slavery under the Dutch was comparatively mild. The Dutch West India Company in 1644 manumitted eleven Negro slaves who had been long in its service. It is interesting to take their names from the record, if for no other reason than that they shed an additional light on the original eleven. The names of those manumitted because they had "served the Company seventeen or eighteen years" and had been "long since promised their freedom on the same footing as other free peoples here in New Netherland" were: Paul d'Angola, Big Manuel, Little Manuel, Manuel de Gerrit de Rens, Simon Congo, Anthony Portuguese, Gracia, Peter Santome, John Francisco, Little Anthony, John Fort Orange. The manumission of these eleven slaves marked a cardinal epoch in the history of the Negro in New York— the beginning of a colony of black freemen in the midst of slavery. This policy of manumission was followed by numbers of individuals.

Slaves in New Netherland differed but little from indentured servants. They had almost full freedom of motion and assembly; they were allowed to marry; wives and daughters had legal protection against the lechery of masters, and they had the right to acquire and hold property. Slaves in New Netherland never became mere merchandise, nor did the slave system ever reach the dehumanized stage which it reached in the English-speaking colonies and states. Perhaps the system under the Dutch lacked, among other things, sufficient time for development; be that as it may, under the English, slavery in the colony flourished and took on all the harsh and cruel traits of the system farther south. Laws were enacted annulling those few rights which the slaves had possessed, and the most severe restrictions and drastic practices were adopted.

The slaves had been far from content under the soft system of the Dutch. They were continually striving for freedom through manumission. It was upon their own petition that the first group was manumitted. As conditions grew harsher, they tried swifter methods. They escaped to Canada or ran away and took refuge with the Indians. In 1705 the General Assembly found it necessary to pass an act forbidding all Negro slaves from "travelling forty miles above the city of Albany, at or above a place called Sarachtoge [Saratoga], on pain of death," unless accompanied by master or mistress. Later a treaty was made with the Six Nations, in which these Indian tribes agreed to deliver up all Negro slaves that might take refuge among them. Such treaties were never lived up to by the Indians.

The increasing cruelty of slavery was attended by the increasing bitterness and resentment of the slaves, until, driven to the extreme, they struck a blind blow at their oppressors. The blow, of course, was futile; indeed, it was followed by laws and practices still more severe and galling. In striking it, however, the Negro wrote his first full-length page in New York history—and a bloody page it is. The report on the

"Negro Insurrection of 1712" made by Governor Robert Hunter to the Lords of Trade may be paraphrased briefly: On April 6,1712 twenty-three Negro slaves met about midnight in the orchard of one Mr. Cook, in the middle of the town, for the purpose of destroying as many of the inhabitants as they could to revenge themselves for the hard usage they felt they had received from their masters. Some of them were armed with fire-arms, some with swords, and others with knives and hatchets. One of them, Coffee (or Cuffee), slave of one Peter Vantilburg, set fire to an outhouse of his master, whereupon the whole band sallied forth and marched to the fire. News of the fire spread through the town, and a crowd of townspeople flocked to it. The band of insurgents opened fire on the crowd, killing nine citizens and wounding five or six others. Alarm was given. The Governor ordered a detachment from the fort to march against the revolting slaves, but they, under cover of night, made their escape into the woods. The Governor, by placing sentries and having the militia of New York and Westchester counties drive the island, captured all the rebels, except six who preferred suicide to capture. In the "tryal before ye Justices" twenty-seven were condemned. Twenty-one were executed—"some were burnt, others hanged, one broke on the wheele and one hung alive in ye towne." The Governor did not strain his words in saying: "There has been the most exemplary punishment inflicted that could be thought of."

Twenty-nine years later the city was again thrown into a panic by the so-called "conspiracy to burn New York and murder its inhabitants." On March 18, 1741 the fort at what is now the Battery was destroyed by fire. A number of fires followed in quick succession throughout the town. Wild rumours began to fly that the fires were the result of a slave conspiracy to destroy the city and massacre the whites. Negroes were arrested wholesale and put into prison, but no clue to the origin of the fires could be found. The mystery was deepened by the fact that none of the fires was connected with any attempt at violence. A month or so after the burning of the fort, Mary Burton, a white indentured servant to John Hughson, an innkeeper, was called before the grand jury to testify regarding a robbery which, it was alleged, had been planned in her master's place. The jury came to feel that in Mary Burton they had the key to the mystery of the fires. The girl at first refused to give any testimony on that point, but under pressure she told a story that involved three Negroes known as Caesar, Prince, and Coffee (or Cuffee) not only in the robbery, but also in the conspiracy to burn the town, massacre the whites, and make themselves the rulers. She testified that the three had met often at her master's house to lay these plans. In her story she also implicated John Hughson, her master, Sara Hughson, her master's wife, and another white woman, named Peggy Kerry, known as "the Irish beauty," who lived at Hughson's and was the kept mistress of Caesar, having had a child by him. It cannot be known how trustworthy Mary Burton's testimony was, but through it scores of persons were eventually involved in the charge. The trial was held in an atmosphere of apprehension and terror. There were, of course, many persons alive who had vivid recollections of the "Insurrection of 1712." In such an atmosphere justice could not have a breathing chance. Many a time has a legal trial served as a sort of substitute for a Roman circus for New Yorkers, but, without doubt, no other legal show has ever approached this 1741 trial in sensationalism and importance. And it is certain that not only New York but every other slave-holding community in the country was deeply interested in the outcome. So important was this case deemed that Chief Justice Horsmanden, in 1744, published a *Journal of the Proceedings against the*

Conspirators. This volume was republished in England in 1748, and in 1810 it was republished in New York as a *History of the Negro Plot*, a book of nearly four hundred pages. The chief purpose of the book was to justify the drastic punishments that had been meted out.

As a result of the trial eighteen were hanged, fourteen were executed in the manner of one, Tom, who was condemned to be "burned alive with a slow fire until he is dead and consumed to ashes." In addition, seventy-odd Negroes were transported out of the country. Among those hanged were John Hughson and his wife, the white girl, Peggy, and an Englishman, a priest, named John Ury.

After the "Conspiracy of 1741" the state of the Negro in New York sank to the nadir, but in the last quarter of the century a change in sentiment regarding slavery began to make itself felt. The doctrine of the Declaration of Independence was not without some collateral effect upon the status of the black man. During the Revolutionary War the Legislature of New York passed an act granting freedom to all slaves who served in the Army for three years or until honourably discharged. Later a bill was passed providing for two Negro regiments. Coloured men of New York formed a good proportion of the nearly four thousand Negro soldiers that fought in the colonial armies. At the close of the Revolutionary War—to be more precise, according to the census of 1790—there were 25,978 Negroes in the State of New York—21,324 slaves and 4,654 freemen.

TWO

THE SPIRIT OF THE REVOLUTION NOT only wrought in New York a humanization of sentiment regarding slavery and a softening of the condition of the slave, but also aroused and strengthened a considerable section of public opinion and set it in motion against the whole institution. In January 1785, four years after the close of the war, nineteen men met and organized the "Society for the Promotion of the Manumission of Slaves, and Protecting Such of them as have been or may be Liberated." Among the purposes of the society, as set forth, were those of defending the rights of the blacks and giving them the elements of education. At the second meeting John Jay and Alexander Hamilton were present; and at a meeting held later, Jay was chosen president of the society and Hamilton secretary. The Quakers, it is true, eighteen years earlier had publicly gone on record as opposing slavery. Purchase Quarterly Meeting, in 1767, sent a statement to the yearly meeting held in Flushing propounding the following question: If it is not consistent with Christianity to buy and sell slaves, is it consistent with the Christian spirit to keep those in slavery that we have already in our possession by purchase, gift, or any otherwise? Slave-holding as a question of religion and morals was constantly considered in the meetings of the Quakers, and by 1779 the last slave held by a Friend was set free. The example of the Quakers influenced individuals outside the sect, but it was the formation of the Manumission Society that marked in New York the beginning of an organized anti-slavery effort, general in character and scope.

The Manumission Society at once set for itself the task of having the Legislature pass an act leading to the abolishment of slavery in New York, and continued to work at that task until it was fully accomplished. The Legislature passed an act in 1799 providing for gradual emancipation; the provisions of the act were that every male child born of a slave after July 4, 1799 should be free after twenty-eight years of service to the owner of its mother, and every female child after twenty-five years of such service. The abolition of slavery was continually agitated and several midway measures were adopted. Finally, on July 4, 1827, an act was passed by which all slaves were emancipated and slavery was abolished in the State of New York. By the census of 1830 there were 44,870 free Negroes in New York State, 14,083 of them living in the city.

The reader, however, must not be left to think that New York led the way towards the abolition of slavery in the North; in fact New York was the last of the Northern states, except New Jersey, to emancipate the slaves. But although New York was late in taking the legal step to abolish slavery within the state, it became one of the strongholds of the forces fighting to abolish slavery in the nation, and one of the important stations on the Underground Railroad. Moreover, it became the chief centre of the free Negroes who played an active and effective part in bringing about national abolition. For in the same year in which New York State abolished slavery—in fact, three months before the passage of the act—the first Negro newspaper in the United States made its appearance in New York City. *Freedom's Journal* was its name; and

its name embodied its purpose. *Freedom's Journal* was in every sense
an organ of propaganda. It was established for the sole and definite
purpose of fighting to end slavery and to secure American citizenship
for the Negro. Within the period between the founding of this first
newspaper and the signing of the Emancipation Proclamation some
two dozen newspapers were established and published by Negroes
in various Northern states. All these publications had the same single
aim—the overthrow of slavery. For certain reasons New York was the
most favourable field for these organs of agitation and propaganda. Out
of the whole number published in the country during the abolition
period, twelve were published in New York State, and of these, eight
were published in New York City; the others in Albany, Troy, Syracuse,
and Rochester. It is astounding on glancing backward to see how well
written and edited were the majority of these periodicals. They stated
and pleaded their cause with a logic and an eloquence which seldom
fell below the highest level of the journalism of the period. And yet it
is not, after all, astounding—there was the great cause, the auspicious
time; and, by some curiously propitious means, there were, too, the
men able to measure up to the cause and the time. There were among
the editors of these papers, especially in New York, men of ability and
men of learning. The founder and editor of *Freedom's Journal* was John
B. Russworm. Russworm was a graduate of Bowdoin College—the first
Negro to graduate from a college in the United States. Dr. James McCune
Smith, who edited one of the papers published in New York City, was
educated at the University of Glasgow. The Rev. Henry Highland
Garnett, who edited the *Clarion* of Troy, was the pastor, unbelievable as
it may sound, of a white church in that city. He also had the distinction of
delivering in the House of Representatives at Washington, on Lincoln's
birthday 1865, a memorial address on the adoption by Congress of the

amendment to the Constitution abolishing slavery. The Rev. Samuel Ringgold Ward, who edited the *Impartial Citizen* at Syracuse, was a marvellous orator and for years the pastor of a white Congregational church at Courtlandville. And there was the great Frederick Douglass, who established and edited the *North Star* at Rochester. A half-dozen others were of much more than ordinary training.

These newspapers quickened and united the free Negroes of the North and did a great deal to arouse and influence public opinion against slavery. The free Negroes of the North actually became one of the strongest arguments against slavery. Many of the Negro anti-slavery papers were short-lived. Only one of them survived the period and is alive today. The *Christian Recorder*, established in Philadelphia in 1856, is still published there as the official organ of the African Methodist Episcopal Church. Frederick Douglass's paper was the strongest and most influential of them all. The *North Star* was read not only by coloured people but by many whites and was without question one of the most powerful of all the antislavery publications. Douglass's international fame as an abolitionist and an orator naturally gave his paper great prestige. The *North Star* did long service; it was first issued November 1, 1847, and continued to be published—later as *Frederich Douglass's Paper*—until it was able to announce the emancipation of the slaves. At the outbreak of the Civil War, and even more sanguinely at the emancipation of the slaves, the Negro press felt that the fight had been completely won. The error was pardonable. It was entirely human to regard so great a victory after so long and hard a struggle as conclusive. The end of the Civil War marked the disappearance of the Negro anti-slavery newspaper and the close of the first period of Aframerican journalism.

But the efforts of the free Negroes of New York against slavery were not limited to those made through their newspapers. New York Negroes played an important part in the Underground Railroad system; they made frequent use of organized protest and resorted to the law and the courts whenever they were able. On September 18, 1850 the Fugitive Slave Bill, passed by Congress, became a law, and the first act for its enforcement was done in New York. On the 26th of the same month in which the law became effective an enforcement officer arrived in New York from Baltimore to claim James Hamlet, who, he made affidavit, was a slave belonging to Mary Brown of Baltimore and had made his escape to New York. The United States Commissioner issued, under the Fugitive Slave Law, the warrant that was demanded for the arrest of Hamlet. The warrant was executed and Hamlet was arrested while working as porter in a store at 58 Water Street and taken back to Baltimore. At the same time it was announced that his owner would allow him to be redeemed for eight hundred dollars.

The coloured people of the city at once took action. A mass meeting was called and advertised by a handbill which read:

BLACK MANHATTAN
The Fugitive Slave Bill!
The Panting Slave!
Freemen to be Made Slaves!
Let Every Colored Man and Woman Attend the Great Mass Meeting
to be Held in
Zion Church Church Street corner of Leonard
On Tuesday Evening, October 2, 1850
For Your Liberty, Your Fireside, is in Danger of being Invaded!
Devote this Night to the Question of Your Duty in the Crisis.
Shall we Resist the Proposition? Shall we Defend Liberties?

Shall we be Freemen or Slaves?
By order of the COMMITTEE OF THIRTEEN.

The absence of superstitious fear in having the meeting called by a committee of thirteen was justified; Zion Church, which held about fifteen hundred, was jammed. Speeches were made and resolutions adopted denouncing the law and attacking its constitutionality. But, unlike so many mass meetings, this one did not merely give an occasion for speeches and resolutions. The sum of eight hundred dollars was raised; the first hundred dollars of which was given by a coloured man named Isaac Hollenbeck.

Hamlet's freedom was purchased, and he was brought back to New York amidst the overwhelming rejoicings of the coloured people of the city.

At the close of the Civil War there were more than fifty thousand Negroes in New York State, about fifteen thousand of them living in New York City.

THREE

N O GREAT AMOUNT OF RESEARCH IS required to find that one of the chief reasons for the intelligent and aggressive action of New York Negroes and for their position of leadership during the period between the Revolutionary and the Civil wars lay in education. The history of education among them goes back as far as 1704. As early as that a missionary society founded in England undertook the religious training of the slaves in New York City. This work was carried on for nearly twenty years by Elias Neau, a Frenchman. The instruction was primarily religious, but a number of slaves gained a rudimentary education through being taught the alphabet and how to read the catechism. Several other missionary efforts of a similar kind were begun and carried on down to the beginning of the Revolution.

Secular education for the Negroes of New York began with the establishment of the African Free School, which was founded by the Manumission Society and opened on November 1, 1787. Here again, however, it must be noted that work by the Quakers preceded the work of the Manumission Society. When the Quakers set their slaves free, they made provisions for the education of the black youth. Nor did these provisions for the slaves they had set free fully satisfy their consciences; the Quakers of Purchase settled their emancipated slaves on lands in the town of Harrison, in Westchester County, and there was begun a Negro community of which a vestigium still remains in the northern part of White Plains. Systematic schooling among the Negroes of New York began, however, with the establishment of the African Free School by the Manumission Society in 1787. The school was opened in a single room, and the first classes were taught by Cornelius Davis, who gave up a school for white children to take charge of this school for black children.

The first building for the school was erected on Cliff Street in 1796. In 1797, 1798, and 1800 the Corporation of the city made small grants to the school, and in 1801 the State Legislature appropriated $1,565.78. It is a curious historical fact that the establishment of the African Free School gave the black children of New York a free school some years before there was any such institution for white children. In truth, this school was the precursor of the New York public school system. The Cliff Street building was burnt down in 1814, but the Corporation of the city again came to the aid of the society and made a grant of a lot on William Street near Duane, where a "commodious brick building" was erected, and opened in 1815. African Free School No. 2, with accommodations for five hundred pupils, was built on Mulberry Street near Grand in 1820. By 1834 there were seven of these African free schools, and several coloured men and women had been installed among the teachers.

The schools were well conducted and the instruction was quite thorough. The boys were taught "reading, writing, arithmetic, English grammar, composition, geography, astronomy, use of the globe, and map and linear drawing." The girls, in addition to reading, writing, arithmetic, the elements of English grammar, and geography, were taught plain sewing and knitting. Charles G. Andrews, for many years one of the principals, published a *History of the African Free School*. The little volume tells of a public examination of the pupils that was held on May 7, 1824, upon which a report was made to the Common Council of the City of New York by a committee appointed from that body. In its report the committee said:

> The undersigned having attended an examination of the children of the African Free Schools on the 7th instant, pursuant to the invitation of the trustees of that Institution to the Common Council, beg leave to state, that the exercises consisted of exhibitions in Spelling, Reading, Writing, Arithmetic, Grammar, Geography, and Elocution, and of Needlework in addition to these, on the part of the females. The answers of both boys and girls to questions in the important and useful branches of simple and compound arithmetic, of Grammar, and of general and local Geography, especially that of our own country, were prompt and satisfactory. The performances in writing were neat, and in many instances, highly ornamental. The behavior of the children was orderly and creditable to them and their teachers.

Mr. Andrews also quotes from the comments made in the *Commercial Advertiser* in its issue of May 12, 1824:

> We had the pleasure on Friday of attending the annual examination of the scholars of the New York African Free School, and we are free to confess that we never derived more satisfaction, or felt a deeper interest, in any school

exhibition in our life. The male and female schools . . .
were united on this occasion, and the whole number
present was about six hundred . . . The whole scene was
highly interesting and gratifying. We never beheld a
white school of the same age (of and under the age of
fifteen) in which, without exception, there was more
order, and neatness of dress, and cleanliness of person.
And the exercises were performed with a degree of
promptness and accuracy which was surprising. There
were two or three Southern gentlemen present, and we
should have been pleased had there been many more . . .
We were particularly struck with the appearance of the
female school . . . There was a neatness of dress and person,
a propriety of manner, and an ease of carriage, which
reflected great credit upon themselves and their teacher.

It would be difficult to over-estimate the value of the African free
schools to the Negroes of New York. And it is easy to see that it was due
mainly to them that there was produced in New York City and State a
body of intelligent and well-trained coloured men and women ready to
assume leadership during the great crisis in the history of their race. The
fact that these schools were genuinely free was very important.

In the fight which the New York Negroes waged against slavery,
the coloured churches of the city played an important part, especially
in providing platforms for leaders and places of assembly for the people.
It was not long after the close of the Revolutionary War that the Negro
in New York began organizing his own churches and building his own
houses of worship. The African Methodist Episcopal Zion Church
was organized in New York City in 1796. It was in Zion Church, at the

corner of Church and Leonard streets, that the protest meeting against the extradition of James Hamlet under the Fugitive Slave Law was held. The organization of Baptists, Episcopalians, and Presbyterians followed in quick succession. Even a Negro Reformed Dutch Church was organized in 1826. This, by the way, is not a matter for laughter; there were a good many Negroes in New York who were the descendants of the manumitted slaves of the original Dutch settlers and who retained much of the Dutch training. There are today in New York Negroes bearing the names Van Ransellear, Van Vechten, Van Vrancken, Van Deusen, Van Dyck, Van Horne, Schuyler, and other such honourable Dutch names.

The course pursued by the Negroes of New York with respect to the church has been, as Mary White Ovington points out in *Half a Man*,[1] directly opposite to their course with respect to the schools. It appears that they found it easier to attain to democracy in education than to reach that end in religion. New York Negroes at first attended the white churches. There they were Jim Crowed in the strictest manner. They sat in the galleries or in certain seats designated for them. They were permitted to receive the communion only after all the whites were through. They had no part in church activities. Listening to the preaching of the doctrines of Jesus Christ under such conditions could not long he tolerated by men of any common sense and decency; so the intelligent Negroes in the white churches withdrew and set up their own churches. This gap between white Christianity and black Christianity has constantly widened, until today the accepted general understanding is that coloured people shall not join white churches or white Y.M.C.A.s, or participate in any white Christian movement; and, of course, vice

1. See Mary White Ovington: *Half a Man*, Longnans, Green and Company, New York, 1911.

versa. In education the course has been the reverse: Negroes started in the African free schools. In 1834 all of the schools and property of the Manumission Society were transferred to the Public School Society. Later, in 1858, all of the Negro schools—taught at that time entirely by coloured teachers—were taken over by the newly established Board of Education. We know that as early as 1857 the coloured people had begun a fight against segregation and discrimination in the public schools. By 1884 the public school system had absorbed most of these separate schools; and in that year Grover Cleveland, then Governor of the state, signed a hill disestablishing the three remaining coloured schools as coloured schools and providing that they he "open for the education of pupils for whom admission is sought without regard to race or color." As a result of these developments the great majority of coloured children attended so-called white schools, and many white children attended so-called coloured schools. Governor Theodore Roosevelt in 1900 signed a hill which repealed the law permitting communities in the state to establish separate schools and provided that no person should he refused admission to or he excluded from any public school in the state on ac count of race or colour.

And so it was that the New York Negroes forced their way from the African Free School, started in a single room, through to full equality in the public school system; and with regard not only to pupils hut also to teachers. There are at present more than three hundred coloured teachers in the public schools of the city. The record in religion is directly opposite; Negroes began by attending the white churches, and today, hut for an infinitesimal number of exceptions, there are no coloured members of white churches in New York City.

FOUR

D URING THE PERIOD BETWEEN THE ABOLISHMENT of
slavery in New York State (1827) and its abolishment in the
nation (1863) the condition of the Negro in New York City, as of free
Negroes in all Northern cities, was anomalous and precarious. He was
neither slave nor citizen; he had neither the protection of a master nor
full equality before the law. This had not always been the condition of
free persons of colour. In the earliest decades free Negroes enjoyed
a limited citizenship. They had voted in all of the colonies and states
except Georgia and South Carolina. It was in 1723 that a law was passed
in Virginia denying them the right. Free Negroes voted in Maryland
down to 1783. It was not until 1835 that North Carolina passed a law
forbidding to free persons of colour the right of voting. In New York,
under the original constitution of the state, adopted in 1777, the right
of suffrage was not limited by any distinction of race or colour. The
question of limiting the suffrage to white voters did not definitely come
up until the second constitution was being drafted in 1821. After bitter
debate free Negroes were granted restricted suffrage, based upon the
qualification of the possession of two hundred and fifty dollars' worth
of real property "over and above debts and encumbrances thereon."
New York did not place Negro voters upon the same plane as white

voters until 1874. In the New England states, with the exception of Connecticut, free Negroes voted on the same terms as whites.

The steady forcing down of the status of the free Negro in all parts of the country was impelled mainly by two conditions of fact: the increase of the number of free Negroes, and sporadic insurrections of the slaves. By the census of 1790 there were 59,557 free Negroes in all the states. By 1860 their number had increased to nearly a half-million—487,970. This great increase was brought about in three ways: partly by the abolishment of slavery in Northern states, partly by the flight of slaves to the North, and partly by thrifty and more fortunate Negroes in the slave states purchasing their own freedom and the freedom of others. A great many Negroes gained their freedom by flight. It is estimated that in the thirty years before the Civil War more than forty thousand of them passed northward through the Underground Railroad stations in the state of Ohio alone.

The number of those who were thrifty and fortunate enough to secure their freedom in the slave states was much larger than is generally supposed. By the census of 1860, there were 95,073 free Negroes in Maryland and the District of Columbia; there were 58,042 in Virginia; 30,463 in North Carolina; 18,647 in Louisiana; and even in darkest Mississippi there were 773.

The proportion of free Negroes to slaves had actually decreased; nevertheless, the black freemen, a wholly negligible element at the close of the eighteenth century, increased to such a degree in intelligence and power that in the second quarter of the following century they had become a problem. They had become not only a problem to be dealt with through a policy of curtailing rights and privileges, but even a menace—a menace to slavery, to be met by rigorous measures of repression and reprisal. A number of intelligent and talented free

Negroes in the North became effective anti-slavery agitators. They were among the earliest of those who sought to organize public opinion against slavery and secure action for its destruction. *Freedom's Journal* was founded in New York by Negro agitators in 1827, four years before the appearance of William Lloyd Garrison's Liberator, and six years before the organization of the American Anti-Slavery Society. They worked not only among their own people; a dozen or more of them were famed and popular orators on white platforms. Fully half of the latter were New Yorkers. Frederick Douglass, Samuel Ringgold Ward, Henry Highland Garnett, Alexander Crummell, James W. C. Pennington, and three or four others spoke not only in this country but also in England, where they helped to kindle anti-slavery sentiment. The last three named were well-educated men. Garnett finished his education at Oneida Institute (New York), Crummell studied at Cambridge University (England), and Pennington had a degree conferred on him by the University of Heidelberg.

It is not difficult to understand the effectiveness of these black men before white audiences. Slavery existed, and here stood these sons of slaves making powerful appeals with unanswerable logic and impassioned eloquence for their millions of brothers held in chains and bought and sold, not in Africa or in some far-off corner of the earth, but here in the United States of America. It was sufficient for the great Frederick Douglass, who gained his freedom by flight, to stand before such an audience and exclaim: "I was a slave! Am I not a man?" Nor were all the noted black agitators men. One of the best of them all—white or black—was a woman, Sojourner Truth. Sojourner was born a slave in Ulster County, New York, about 1798, and was called Isabella. She became a freewoman when the state abolished slavery. She drifted to New York City, where, after having a vision one night, she rose up and announced herself Sojourner Truth: Sojourner because the Lord had commanded her to travel up and down the land, and Truth because she was to declare the truth to the people. And a name of what beauty she evolved! Sojourner Truth was one of the most effective speakers of the Anti-Slavery Society. She was pure black, and a very tall and striking figure. Her deep voice and mystical manner seemed to have an almost miraculous effect on her hearers. She was a fervent anti-slavery agitator, but her appeal was broader than the question of slavery; it embraced women's rights. Sojourner Truth was a strong factor in the woman's suffrage movement. She was present at the second National Woman's Suffrage Convention held in Akron, Ohio, in 1852, and made a memorable speech. The "Libyan Sibyl," as she was often called, because of her reputed oracular powers and her sublime faith, was a source of inspiration and confidence for the Negro radicals with whom she worked. At a meeting of the leaders held during the war, at which Frederick Douglass was speaking, there was little but pessimism and gloom. Sojourner Truth instantaneously changed the atmosphere of the meeting by interrupting Douglass and thundering out: "Frederick, is God dead?"

But the free Negroes did not confine their efforts to agitation. They acted. All along the northern bank of the Ohio River and in New York, Philadelphia, and some other Northern cities, Underground Railroad stations were maintained, and Negroes took active part in conducting them. Some intrepid ones ventured into the South and urged and assisted slaves to make their escape, guiding them by the Star of the North. And even in this hazardous work all were not men. No one was bolder or more skillful in it than Harriet Tubman, who stands out heroic in character and deeds. Born a slave in Maryland, she escaped in 1849, when she was perhaps twenty-two or twenty- three years old, and made her way to New York. She made nineteen trips into the South and assisted more than one hundred slaves in making their escape. She was a confidante of John Brown. Wendell Phillips relates that the last time he ever saw John Brown was when the latter came to his house and brought Harriet Tubman, saying: "Mr. Phillips, I bring you one of the best and bravest persons on this continent—General Tubman, as we call her." She was several times a guest at the home of Ralph Waldo Emerson. Her work was known and feared by the slave-owners, and at one time there was an aggregate reward of forty thousand dollars offered by Maryland slaveholders for her capture. Because of her daring and experience she was employed in the secret service of the Union Army during the war. After the war Harriet established an old folks' home for Negroes on a piece of property that, in 1857, William H. Seward had sold her near his home at Auburn, New York. She lived to be more than eighty years old and was strong and vigorous up to her death.

Contrary to the common idea that the Negro was wholly docile and submissive in slavery is the fact that almost from the beginning he made repeated efforts to throw off his bonds by force. There were thirty-odd definite attempts at insurrection, the earliest dating back into the seventeenth century. The first serious insurrection of slaves was attempted in New York City, in 1712. It was this insurrection that sent the first quiver of apprehension through the colonies. It was also in New York that was planned the second attempt at revolt, which made the whole country shudder. This was the plot of 1741, already spoken of, and termed by Benjamin Brawley in his *Social History of the American Negro* "in some ways the most important single event in the history of the Negro in the Colonial Period." All the other slave rebellions of importance took place in the South.

As early as 1722 an armed body of some two hundred slaves

gathered near the mouth of the Rappahannock River in Virginia to carry out a plan to kill their masters while they were assembled at church. The plot was discovered and frustrated. Slaves in South Carolina armed themselves and broke into open rebellion in 1730 and again in 1739. They burnt houses and killed a number of whites, but themselves suffered the greater loss. The first truly formidable uprising in the South was the Cato Insurrection in South Carolina near Charleston in 1740. Under the leadership of a slave named Cato, an armed band of Negroes marched for miles burning and killing. They killed a score of white people before they were subdued by the militia.

The chief effect of these earlier insurrections was to frighten the masters and make the lot of the slaves harder through severer regulations. There was little or no effect upon the condition of free Negroes for the reason that their number was, at the time, too insignificant. But later slave insurrections directly affected the status of free Negroes, north and south. Three of these insurrections had far-reaching results. In 1800 came the Gabriel Insurrection in Virginia. A thousand slaves, led by Gabriel, himself a slave, planned to seize the city of Richmond. The plan was well laid and contemplated the capture of the arsenal and storehouse. On the day set for the uprising a devastating storm, which swept away bridges and inundated roads, burst over the section, and the greater part of those involved in the plot found it impossible to reach the rendezvous. Most of those who did assemble were daunted by superstitious fears. In the meantime Richmond was apprised of the revolt and placed under arms. Gabriel and thirty-five others were executed.

In 1822 the better-known and better-planned Denmark Vesey Insurrection was attempted in South Carolina. Vesey was a man of superior intelligence and of some education. As a boy and young man he had travelled as a sailor. He could read and write, and spoke French as well as English. In 1800, when he was thirty-three, he purchased his freedom for six hundred dollars. As a freeman he worked at the carpenter's trade in Charleston and accumulated a sum of money. His spare time he devoted to study. Vesey continued for twenty years to work and study, all the while reflecting upon his condition as a black freeman and upon the condition of his fellow blacks who were slaves. He knew what the Negroes of Haiti had done, for he had been there; and a plan for the Negroes in and around Charleston to do something similar slowly matured in his mind. Late in the year 1821 he sounded out and broached his plan to two Negroes in the city. Before the end of the year the band of conspirators numbered six. For seven months the work of organizing the Negroes, slave and free, inside the city and for miles around, went on with unbelievable secrecy. Vesey's plan, in brief, was to seize Charleston, wipe out the whites, and free the blacks. Arms were cautiously purchased and pikes were manufactured. The plotters were, of course, relying on the arsenal for their real supply of arms. They were extremely careful about what blacks they approached. One of the rules adopted was that no personal servants should be enlisted. Organization was carried on with the aid of cabbalistic words and numbers. Secrecy was so well guarded that the officials of the city were completely deceived about preparations that had been going on for months under their eyes. After a leak of information reached the officials, two of Vesey's lieutenants, Peter Poyas and Mingo Harth, were placed under temporary arrest. But they exhibited such extraordinary sang-froid and so laughed at the idea of a slave insurrection that they were released. Another of Vesey's leaders, Ned Bennett, hearing that his name had been mentioned, went voluntarily before the officials and demanded an examination. Of cool courage history has no finer examples to offer. Events justified the wisdom of the rule to enlist no personal servants; and had it been strictly adhered to, the story would have ended differently. But the whole plot was revealed two days before the date set for action—and by a household servant. Denmark Vesey and thirty-four others were executed, and forty-three were deported. Vesey before his arrest destroyed all his records and lists of names and died without betraying a single secret or associate.

The best-known and the most significant of these slave revolts of the nineteenth century was the Nat Turner Insurrection in Virginia, in 1831. This was also the last serious attempt. Among the slaves of Virginia that lived near the edge of the Dismal Swamp was one, a short, powerful black man, named Nat Turner. There was no similarity between Nat Turner and Denmark Vesey, though both of them by similar actions wrote their names in American history. Vesey was a cultured man, and his influence over his followers was intellectual. Turner, a naturally intelligent man, but illiterate, swayed his followers through an influence that was mystical. He was a plantation preacher and gave himself to fasting and prayer. He communed with the spirits and saw visions. He was held as a prophet by the blacks and regarded with superstitious respect by the whites. Vesey appealed to the manhood of his followers. Once when he rebuked a fellow Negro for bowing low to a white man, the Negro said: "We are slaves." Vesey retorted: "You deserve to be." Nat Turner gathered his followers and inspired them to act by "command of God." On the eve of action he is recorded as saying to them:

> Friends and brothers, we are to commence a great work tonight. Our race is to be delivered from bondage, and God has appointed us as the men to do His bidding; and let us be worthy of our calling. I am told to slay all the whites we

encounter, men, women, and children. Remember we do not go forth for the sake of blood and carnage, but it is necessary that in the commencement of this revolution all the whites we meet must die; until we have an army strong enough to carry on the war upon a Christian basis.

Turner attempted to carry out the command fully. He and his band, starting in the night, marched from plantation to plantation, dealing death and destruction, sparing no person with a white skin. They destroyed much property and killed more than sixty whites, including a number of children, before they were subdued. They fought a pitched fight with a detachment of militia and United States troops in which more than a hundred of the band were killed. The others fled to the Dismal Swamp. Nat Turner and others were captured, and together with him twenty were hanged.

Each of these forerunners of John Brown—even as he—failed. In the nature of things, they could not succeed. The blacks of Haiti might conquer the handful of white overlords on the island and, at that time, keep the others off; but the situation of the slaves in the United States was absolutely different. Yet these abortive attempts for freedom— even as John Brown's—produced vital and far-reaching results. In no instance did they gain freedom for any slave; rather, they served to bind the chains of slavery tighter. Restrictions more rigid than ever were placed upon the slaves. Even the privilege of religious assembly—an ancient one—was all but abolished. The slave-owners were as vitally affected as the slaves. They became apprehensive and panicky. The spectre of murder and massacre came to haunt them, a spectre they were never entirely able to lay.

But the free Negro was the class most vitally affected. In the

South the rigid regulations laid down for the slaves were applied to the freemen and, naturally, bore upon them harder. All over the South and through the North sentiment against them grew. In the South they were a menace. In the North they became a problem, a combined moral and social problem—and there are few things in the world more annoying. They were regarded with irritation, suspicion, and hatred. In 1827 Henry Clay, then Secretary of State, said in a public address: "Of all classes of our population, the most vicious is that of the free coloured." The weight of sentiment of this sort fell heavily upon the free Negroes of New York, constituting, as they did, the largest body of intelligent and aggressive Negroes in the country.

FIVE

T HIS TIDE OF ANTAGONISTIC SENTIMENT WHICH swept over the free Negroes gave acceleration to a movement that brought upon those in New York and other cities in the North a struggle second in importance to the struggle against slavery. That movement was the colonization of free Negroes. Colonization was not a new idea. It had for some time been considered by philanthropic people as a plan for helping the blacks who were free. Certain of the Quakers put it into effect on a small scale by purchasing lands on which to settle their manumitted slaves in communities of their own. It grew from the plan for isolated Negro communities to that of settlement in a territory set apart in the western section of the country, then to colonization in the West Indies. A number of prominent people suggested Africa. In 1811 Thomas Jefferson strongly endorsed the idea of African colonization.

But African colonization got little further than an expression of ideas until action was taken by a Negro. He was Paul Cuffee, a freeman of colour of New Bedford, Massachusetts. Cuffee was a sailor, who finally became master of his own ship, and who in his career saw a good part of the world. He also made money; when he died he left an estate of twenty thousand dollars. He was converted to colonization and in

1815 transported in his own ship nine Negro families, thirty-eight persons, to the west coast of Africa at a cost of four thousand dollars all of which he bore. Cuffee's undertaking attracted the attention of the country and caused ideas about colonization to take on definite form. In December 1816 a meeting of those interested in colonization was called in Washington, and an organization was formed to be known as the American Society for Colonizing Free People of Color of the United States. Henry Clay, then Speaker of the House of Representatives, presided at this meeting. The Colonization Society approached the Government for support, and in 1819 Congress, upon a recommendation from President Monroe, passed a bill appropriating a hundred thousand dollars that could be used for the purposes of the society. This co-operation between the Government and the Colonization Society resulted in the establishment of the colony of Liberia, on the west coast of Africa. Liberia in 1847 became an independent Negro republic, with the seat of government at Monrovia, named in honour of President Monroe.

From its inception the Colonization Society was an amalgam of diverse ideas and ideals. It was all things to all men. It furnishes the only instance in American history in which groups holding conflicting opinions on the polymorphous Negro question united for a common end; and, stranger still, each group felt that it was realizing its intention. The common end was the transporting of the free Negroes out of the United States. Working side by side were those who were moved by a sincere desire to ameliorate the Negro's condition; those who wished only to rid themselves of all moral and social responsibility for a troublesome situation; and those who were determined to banish forever what they considered a threat to the security of the slave system. The only group interested in the Negro not to affiliate was the abolitionist group. And at no time did the Colonization Society attack slavery, even in the mildest manner.

The efforts of the society, so far as its main object was concerned, were futile. The organization increased rapidly in membership and wealth, and branches were established in Northern and Southern states, but the results of its work to get free Negroes out of the country were less than negligible. In thirteen years after the first shipment in 1820 only 2,885 emigrants had been sent to Liberia. Nor could any amelioration of the condition of the race be noted. On the contrary, the efforts of the society had a disastrous effect. The propaganda that it spread emphasized the utter hopelessness, despair, and defeat for the Negro in America. It declared that he could never become an enlightened and useful citizen of the United States, and that his only hope for opportunity and development lay in the establishment of a country for him in Africa. (It will be noted as we go further that this was the identical doctrine and argument of Garvey in the "Back to Africa" movement one hundred years later.) Nor did the propaganda stop at this point. It was often direct vilification of the free Negroes. It was at the tenth annual meeting of the society that Henry Clay expressed his opinion of free coloured people quoted on a previous page.

The Denmark Vesey and Nat Turner insurrections brought added strength and wealth to the Colonization Society and gave it grounds for doubling and redoubling its efforts; nevertheless, emigration to Liberia languished. In the twenty years from 1833 to 1853 the organization, with all the influence and money it had behind it, sent out less than four thousand settlers. The fundamental reason for the failure of the colonization scheme was a very patent one; it was simply that the free Negroes would not go to Africa. They not only refused to go; they fought the plans of the Colonization Society from the start. In fact, the first national convention of Negroes held in the United States met in Philadelphia in 1831 for the express purpose of opposing "the operations and misrepresentations of the American Colonization Society in these United States." The convention, speaking on behalf of the free Negroes of the country, stated that "the inevitable tendency of this [the society's] doctrine was to strengthen their enemies and retard their [the free Negroes'] advancement in morals, literature, and science; in short to extinguish the last glimmer of hope and throw an impenetrable gloom over their former and more reasonable prospects." In 1834 the meeting was held in New York.

At the beginning of the second half of the nineteenth century there was a recrudescence of agitation for colonization, and at this time a number of free Negroes in Northern cities, disheartened by unyielding pressure, came out in favour of emigration. Some of them advocated Africa, some Central America, and others Haiti. The advocates of Haiti eventually succeeded in taking about two thousand settlers to the Black Republic. But the big majority of the Northern leaders continued to oppose the whole idea. The New York group, led by Frederick Douglass, fought it with all their might. Douglass ridiculed it, saying that before a ship could make the return trip, there would be ten shiploads of new babies waiting on the dock.

The Negroes in New York not only had to bear the pressure of general sentiment against free Negroes, but were called on to stand up under an economic pressure stronger than that endured by any other of the free groups. For generations the New York Negroes had had an almost uncontested field in many of the gainful occupations. They were domestic servants, labourers, boot-blacks, chimney-sweeps, whitewashers, barbers, hotel waiters, cooks, sailors, stevedores, seamstresses, ladies' hairdressers, janitors, caterers, coachmen. (At that time a black coachman was almost as sure a guarantee of aristocracy for a Northern white family as a black mammy for a family of the South.) In a limited way they were engaged in the skilled trades. The United States census of 1850 lists New York Negroes in fourteen trades. In two occupations—as janitors of business buildings and as caterers—a number of individuals actually grew wealthy. At one time the best food that could be procured in New York City was that furnished by coloured caterers. In the decade 1830–40 a favourite resort for bankers, brokers, and merchants was a restaurant kept by a coloured man, Thomas Downing, on Broad Street near Wall. He made a fortune. In that same period the most exclusive parties and most fashionable weddings were served by a coloured caterer, Thomas Jackson. Jackson in his day was the arbiter of New York in things gustatory. Fraunces's Tavern, at Broad and Pearl streets, now one of the great historic landmarks in New York City, was for many generations the most famous tavern in New York. It was established by Samuel Fraunces, a coloured man from an island of the French West Indies, familiarly known as Black Sam. Fraunces bought the property in 1762 for two thousand pounds. It was at Fraunces's Tavern that the body now known as the New York Chamber of Commerce was organized, in 1768. The inn was frequented by General Washington, and it was there that he bade farewell to his officers, on December 4, 1783. The farewell dinner was tendered by Governor Clinton. It was a dinner that was well washed down, the bill rendered by Fraunces to Governor Clinton for liquors amounting to ninety-seven pounds, twelve shillings. Fraunces personally conducted the tavern for a number of years. He was well known and well liked by the most prominent New York citizens of his day. His daughter, Phoebe, was Washington's housekeeper at the mansion which the Commander-in-Chief occupied as headquarters in New York in 1776. When Washington became President, he made

Fraunces steward of what was then the White House, in New York, located at Number 3 Cherry Street. He remained in Washington's employ in New York and in Philadelphia until 1796 or later, as shown by receipts signed by Fraunces, one of which is now on exhibition at the tavern.

Fraunces's Tavern was purchased and restored as a memorial, in 1905, by the Sons of the Revolution.

The New York Negroes as a class were industrious and thrifty and were making economic gains; then began the wave of foreign immigration, which continued to swell until, economically, it all but submerged them. In the ten years prior to 1830 less than a hundred and thirty thousand immigrants entered the United States. In the fifteen years between 1830 and 1845 nearly a million entered. In the fifteen years between 1845 and 1860 there were nearly four million. Foreign immigration bore down particularly hard on the New York Negro because so large a proportion of the immigrants came into the port of New York—and remained there. The struggle was waged chiefly in the wider fields of domestic service, common labour, and the so-called menial jobs. Gradually but steadily the Negro lost ground. There is, however, an interesting instance of survival that merits mention. In 1825 two Negroes set up the firm of Jackson and Smith, chimney-sweeps. The firm has come down through three generations and exists today as George Smith and Son, specialists on defective chimneys and experts on chimney construction and ventilation.

At the beginning of the second half of the last century the condition of the New York Negro was in many ways at its worst. And this aggressive group felt keenly the sentiment, the acts, the humiliations and insults, that they had to contend against. In the middle of the last century Negroes were not allowed to ride in the street-cars in New

York, except in certain cars bearing a sign that ran along their length: "Colored People Allowed in This Car." This particular humiliation was brought to an end in 1854 by a courageous coloured woman, a teacher in one of the Negro public schools, who on being ordered out of a car clung to her seat until she was dragged out. She took her case into the courts and, with Chester A. Arthur as one of her lawyers, won it. And so against the New York Negro, out of the fierce economic struggle in which he was forced to engage in the face of great odds, came a new antagonism—the antagonism of those who were competing with him for bread and which later was to manifest itself in a bloody riot.

SIX

THE UNITED STATES SUPREME COURT IN 1857 handed down the momentous Dred Scott decision, the culmination of all the legal devices of the pro-slavery forces to make the slave system secure and permanent. Dred Scott was a slave in Missouri whose master had on several occasions taken him into free territory. Back in Missouri, Scott brought suit to gain his liberty on the ground that he had lost his status as a slave through his residence in territory where slavery was prohibited. After nearly ten years of litigation his case reached the Supreme Court and was there decided. The decision, which was rendered by Chief Justice Taney, not only settled the issue raised by Scott, but went far beyond and attempted to make every foot of American soil safe for the slave-holder. It opened up the vast western section to slavery by declaring that Congress had no constitutional authority to abolish slavery in the territories. And it dealt a direct and staggering blow to the free coloured people by laying down the brazen and ruthless doctrine that the Negro "had no rights which the white man was bound to respect."

The Dred Scott decision proved to be the beginning of the end of slavery. History-changing events followed in portentous succession. In 1859 John Brown was at Harpers Ferry. In 1860 Abraham Lincoln was nominated by the newly organized Republican party. In 1861 Fort Sumter was fired upon, and the "irrepressible conflict," so many times a prophecy in the orations of William H. Seward, became a reality. Again the Negroes of New York were thrown directly into the vortex of a national convulsion. Above all Northern cities, New York was the Mecca of the Southern planters. To go to Philadelphia or Boston might never enter their minds, but they came frequently and in large numbers to New York. At the outbreak of the Civil War Southern slave-holding interests owed the merchants of New York something like two hundred million dollars, a sum which the business interests of the city had no desire of losing, even for the most patriotic end. These were two of the reasons why pro-slavery sentiment was strong in New York City.

But the Negroes of New York hailed the war, and the leaders redoubled their efforts against slavery. They began immediately to importune the Government for the right and chance to do their share of the fighting. Frederick Douglass centred his energies on this objective. At the beginning of the war, however, the Administration at Washington and the Union commanders in the field feared the proposal, and general sentiment in the North was opposed to it. But certain federal generals in the field began utilizing Negroes. In May 1862 Colonel Thomas Wentworth Higginson was organizing and drilling a regiment of former slaves in South Carolina. In the fall of 1862 General Butler organized a Negro regiment in Louisiana. The formation of other units followed, and before the end of 1862 four Negro regiments were on the fighting line. But it was not until after the issuance of the Emancipation Proclamation that Lincoln authorized the raising of Negro troops, and the Negroes of the North were given the chance for which they had long been clamouring. When the Negro troops regularly entered the

Union armies, they were badly needed. The fortunes of war had swayed back and forth. The initial enthusiasm and confidence of the North had perceptibly waned. The realization had come that the struggle would be long and hard. Grant had captured Fort Donelson; Lee had been held at Antietam; but the Union had not yet gained a decisive victory— Gettysburg and Vicksburg were in the unknown future—and the final outcome was still in doubt. Volunteering had ceased to be spontaneous, and the Government had been driven to conscription.

Immediately following the Proclamation (January 1, 1863) Negro volunteers rushed into the Army. Their first regiment was the Fifty-fourth Massachusetts, organized February 9, 1863. In all, one hundred and sixty-one regiments of Negro troops, approximately one hundred and eighty thousand men, fought in the Civil War. These forces included one hundred and forty-one regiments of infantry, seven of cavalry, twelve of heavy and one of light artillery. New York furnished four of these regiments. The enlistment of coloured soldiers had a decided effect on the Negro and the nation. More and more, as the war went on, the truth emerged that under the ostensible issue of preserving the Union was the fundamental issue of abolishing slavery. White men who were happy to fight and die to the slogan: "Save the Union!" were not so moved to sacrifice by the task of freeing the slaves. But sentiment for the Negro and his cause was strengthened by the fact that black men were fighting and dying both to save the Union and to free the slaves. And by the same fact new strength and dignity were given to the Negro leaders in the North. They were given an unshakable foundation on which to base further demands. And further demands they continued to make. For while the coloured people as a whole may have felt that with emancipation and the war won by the Union their racial troubles would be at an end, many of the leaders were wise enough to foresee that there would be questions still unsettled and dangers still existent. In October 1864 a National Convention of Colored Men met in Syracuse, New York, and for four days discussed these questions and dangers. Frederick Douglass, who presided, was emphatic in pointing out that the Proclamation was a war measure and might not be regarded as a legal abolishment of slavery when civil authority was restored. In fact, slavery was not actually abolished until the Thirteenth Amendment to the Constitution was adopted.

The leaders were sustained in their demands by the manner in which the Negro troops acquitted themselves. Before the end of the war "The colored troops fought nobly" became a much quoted phrase. They took part in a number of important battles and made an impression on the General of the Armies of the Union which that most taciturn man gave expression to in a commendation during the skirmishes around Richmond. Negro troops under General Burnside had mined a Confederate fort, and the General wished to give them the lead in the charge that was planned to follow the explosion. The distinction was finally given to white troops. On the failure of the enterprise General Grant commented: "General Burnside wanted to put his colored division in front; I believe if he had done so it would have succeeded."

Conscription was nowhere popular, but in New York City it was met with open hostility and violence. For four days in July 1863 the Draft Riots raged and the city was in the hands of a mob against which the police were powerless. After demolishing draft headquarters the mob proceeded to wreak vengeance upon Negroes wherever found. They were chased and beaten and killed—hanged to trees and lamp posts. Thousands fled the city, hiding themselves "on the outskirts of the city, in the swamps and woods back of Bergen, New Jersey, at

Weeksville, and in the barns and outhouses of the farmers of Long Island and Morrisania"; and hundreds sought refuge in the police stations. A historian of the time gives this description:

> The sight of one in the streets would call forth a halloo as when a fox breaks cover, and away would dash a crowd of men in pursuit . . . At one time there lay at the corner of 27th Street and Seventh Avenue the dead body of a Negro, stripped nearly naked, and around it a collection of Irishmen dancing or shouting like wild Indians . . . The hunt for these poor creatures became so fearful, and the impossibility to protect them in their scattered localities so apparent, that they were received into the police stations. But this soon proved inadequate and they were taken to the arsenal where they could be protected against the mob. Here the poor creatures were gathered by hundreds and slept on the floor and were regularly fed by the authorities.[1]

The Colored Orphan Asylum occupied a block on Fifth Avenue between Forty-third and Forty-fourth streets. More than two hundred children were housed there in a wooden building four stories high. The insatiate mob marched against this institution. The superintendent and matrons, who had been watching through hours of terror, hastily led the inmates out by the rear as the mob entered through the front. In a few moments the building was in flames. The children, at first quartered in the police stations, were finally gathered up, and, with a strong guard of police at the front and rear and a detachment of soldiers on either side,

1 J. T. Headley: *The Great Riots of New York City.*

they toddled down to the foot of East Thirty-fifth Street and were taken aboard ferryboats to Blackwell's Island, where they were given a refuge. In the Draft Riots more than a thousand persons were killed and wounded, and something like a million dollars' worth of property was destroyed.

The reaction from the Draft Riots was a flood of kindly feeling towards the Negro and of indignation against the mob. Within a few months a regiment of Negro troops, raised and equipped by the Union League Club, marched down Broadway on their way to the front escorted by leading citizens and cheered by thousands that lined the sidewalks.

After the close of the war the arena for the Negro shifted from the North to the South. The freedmen, rather than the freemen of colour, came to be the centre of discussion and the object of action. The controversies in Congress and throughout the country surged round the war amendments to the Constitution, Reconstruction, and the civil rights bills, with the four million ex-slaves as the centre of the storm. Their status and future became the chief concern of the nation, so far as it was concerned with the Negro. The Negroes of the North dropped into a place of insignificance from which they did not completely emerge until the United States entered the World War. Large numbers of educated Northern Negroes joined the "carpet-bag" migration to the South and played an important part in political leadership and the social advancement of the freedmen. Many of the first teachers in schools for Negro children established in the South were educated coloured women from the North. In the rapid progress of the former slaves—at emancipation illiterate, penniless, and homeless—the work of the Northern Negroes who went South was a vital force.

A pause now set in upon the racial activities of the Negroes of the North. They had been among the chief agitators for freedom. They in themselves had been the greatest argument that the Negro should be free. They had stood upon the vantage-ground from which they could render aid to their brothers in bondage. Now the slaves were free. They had been made citizens and given the ballot and were exercising political power. The whole scene and the spotlight had shifted down to Washington and below the Potomac. Othello's occupation was gone. It was years before the Negroes in the North fully realized that the close of the Civil War marked only the first great step in the Negro's fight for complete freedom, and that they again would have to take the lead. This hiatus was particularly marked in New York. For nearly fifty years this city had been the principal centre of the free Negro radicals. It was the stage on which most of the brilliant and powerful Negro leaders had played their parts. It was to New York City that Frederick Douglass first came when he escaped from slavery in 1838, and it was in his adopted state of New York that he rose to world fame and the unquestioned leadership of his race.

It is probable that the migration of Fred Douglass, as the coloured people loved to call him, had something to do with the lethargic state that settled upon New York. At the close of the Civil War Douglass had achieved a greatness in world affairs paralleled in modern history by only one other man of African blood—Toussaint L'Ouverture. Not yet fifty, he was a tall, straight, magnificent man, with a leonine head covered with a mass of hair, which later became a glistening white mane. In ability and appearance he was a leader of men. His name was known in every civilized country. Douglass, the escaped slave, was the incarnation of all the arguments against slavery. For twenty-five years as agitator, editor, organizer, counsellor, eloquent advocate, and fearless champion he had worked for freedom and equality for his race. He had been the associate of all the great abolitionists, and the friend and adviser of

Lincoln. From its beginning he had been a force in the woman's suffrage movement, realizing that it was a kindred cause to Negro freedom. He had been a confidant and helper of John Brown. Papers found on John Brown when he was captured at Harpers Ferry involved Douglass, and the black leader fled to Canada, thence to England, just in time to avoid arrest under a requisition issued by Governor Wise of Virginia. He returned the following year and supported Lincoln for the presidency. It is not difficult to conclude that his absence from the state caused a gap in the civic life of the Negro in New York.

Douglass went to Washington to live, but retained his New York citizenship. In 1872 he was named elector at large on the presidential ticket by the Republican party in New York, and upon Grant's election was chosen to take the electoral vote of the state to Washington. It was also in 1872 that the convention of the Equal Rights party met in New York City and nominated Victoria C. Woodhull for president of the United States, and Frederick Douglass for vice-president. In Washington, Douglass received many political honours. President Grant appointed him secretary of the Santo Domingo Commission, which was sent to negotiate a treaty with the Island Republic for its annexation to the United States. In turn he held the positions of Councillor of the District of Columbia, Marshal of the District of Columbia, Recorder of Deeds for the District of Columbia, and Minister to Haiti. It was in 1869 that he moved to Washington, and there for a quarter of a century longer he remained, unrivalled, the outstanding figure of his race. He was referred to as "the Sage of Anacostia." His old homestead, Anacostia, is now a Negro shrine, maintained by the National Association of Colored Women's Clubs. It was restored through the efforts of Mrs. Mary B. Talbert of Buffalo, New York, one time president of the association. He died in 1895 in his seventy-eighth year. Six months after his death

Booker T. Washington made his famous Atlanta speech, and a new leader suddenly stood before the people.

Douglass died, probably, a disappointed man. He had lived to see many of the highest hopes for his race fall to the ground. He was a philosopher, but there were many things he saw come to pass that he could hardly have accepted with resignation. He had seen the Negro disfranchised and all the guarantees of equal citizenship fought for and laid down for him in the fundamental law of the land flouted. He had seen the race made the victim of new hatreds and brutalities not equalled under some phases of slavery. He had the knowledge that in the ten years before his death more than two thousand of his fellows had been lynched and tortured and burnt at the stake.

As long as there are American Negroes Frederick Douglass will be remembered, but he will be remembered and honoured chiefly for the prodigious things he accomplished as a Negro in New York.

SEVEN

I N THE EARLIEST DAYS THE NEGRO population of New York
lived, naturally, in and about the city at the tip of Manhattan Island.
In the middle of the last century they lived mainly in the vicinity of
Lispenard, Broome, and Spring streets. When Washington Square was
the centre of fashionable life, large numbers of Negroes engaged in
domestic service in the homes of the rich lived in a fringe of nests to
the west and south of the square. As late as 1880 the major portion of
the Negro population of the city lived in Sullivan, Bleecker, Thompson,
Carmine, and Grove streets, Minetta Lane, and adjacent streets. It is
curious to see that some of these nests still persist. Scattered through
Greenwich village and "Little Italy," small groups of Negroes may be
found who have never lived in any other part of the city. Negro New
York has passed on and left them stranded and isolated. They are vestiges
of a generation long gone by. They appear to be content, however, and
probably they view with some scorn the new and rather raw Harlem
centre. And they have some ground for sectional pride, for they show,
perhaps, as large a percentage of New-York-born adults as any other
section of the city. Mary White Ovington in a social study that she made
inquired into the places of birth of 1,036 Negro tenement-dwellers in
the five sections of Manhattan where coloured people at the time lived.

Fifty-seven per cent of the adults in the Greenwich Village section who were questioned were born in New York City.[1] By 1890 the centre of the coloured population had shifted to the upper Twenties and lower Thirties west of Sixth Avenue. Ten years later another considerable shift northward had been made to West Fifty-third Street and to San Juan Hill (West Sixty-first, Sixty-second, and Sixty-third streets). For some decades most of the upper class and well-to-do coloured people had lived in Brooklyn; their exodus from Manhattan had been caused principally by the Draft Riots. A large number of them owned homes there, and Brooklyn was the centre of social life and respectability.

I have indicated that during the fourth quarter of the last century there was a pause in the racial activities of the Negroes in the North. It would be more strictly true to say that there was a change in activities. In New York the Negro now began to function and express himself on a different plane, in a different sphere; and in a different way he effectively impressed himself upon the city and the country. Within this period, roughly speaking, the Negro in the North emerged and gained national notice in three great professional sports: horse-racing, baseball, and prize-fighting. He also made a beginning and headway on the theatrical stage. And New York, the New York of the upper Twenties and lower Thirties west of Sixth Avenue, became the nucleus of these changed activities.

Horse-racing as an American sport reached development first in the South. The Southern landowners and aristocrats had taken up from the English gentry both riding to hounds and racing early in the last century. By the middle of the century there was local racing on tracks

1. Mary White Ovington: *Half a Man*. Longmans, Green and Company, New York, 1911.

at New Orleans, Mobile, Charleston, Richmond, Nashville, Lexington (Kentucky), and Louisville. The Civil War interrupted the sport; but immediately after the war it was resumed on a grander scale; associations were organized and race-meets were scheduled. This tendency culminated in the building of a great track at Louisville and the offering of large prizes. Then was established the Kentucky Derby, the first American racing classic, an event which each year drew the fancy from all over the country. The Southern horse-owners, naturally—in fact, of necessity—made use of Negro jockeys, trainers, and stable-boys; so there grew up a class of Negro horsemen unequalled by any in the land. When the first Kentucky Derby was run, out of the fourteen jockeys who rode in the race thirteen were coloured. Therefore when the centre of horse-racing was shifted to the East and became, somewhat in the English sense, a national sport, Negro jockeys constituted the very first ranks of the profession. When racing shifted to the East and became also a profitable business venture, with the book-maker as a recognized factor, the great jockeys jumped into national popularity. In the heyday of racing the name of the winner of the Futurity, the Suburban, the Realization, the Brooklyn Handicap, the Metropolitan Handicap, or the Saratoga Cup was as widely heralded and almost as widely known as the name of the winner of a present-day championship prize-fight. In the days when jockeys were popular idols, none were more popular than the best of the coloured ones. No American jockey was ever more popular than Isaac Murphy. All in all, Murphy was the most finished American horseman who ever rode a race. In the Saratoga season of 1882 he won forty-nine of his fifty-one races. In the long history of the Kentucky Derby he is the only jockey that ever rode three winners; he rode the winner in 1884, 1890, and 1891. Four times he rode his mounts to victory in the American Derby, in 1884, 1885,1886, and

1888. There was only one white jockey of his time, "Snapper" Garrison, who could be mentioned with him. Other famous Negro jockeys were: Pike Barnes, Andy Hamilton, Jimmie Winkfield, Willie Simms, Johnny Stoval, "Tiny" Williams, the two Clayton brothers, "Soup" Perkins, "Monk" Overton, Line Jones, Bob Isom, Emanuel Morris, Felix Carr, and Jimmie Lee. To Lee goes the credit for one of the most sensational performances ever carried through by any jockey on any track; at Churchill Downs, Louisville, on June 5, 1907, he won each of the six races on the card. Pike Barnes had the distinction of winning the Futurity the first time it was run, in 1888. His mount was Proctor Knott, on whom he just beat out Andy Hamilton on Salvator. Willie Simms was one of the best jockeys of all time. In a great degree the success of the Dwyer stables was due to his horsemanship. Riding abroad under the Croker-Dwyer colours, he was the first non-English jockey to win a race on an English track. Simms was the first American jockey to shorten his stirrups and introduce the monkey-on-a-stick seat, which was afterwards universally adopted.

The Negro jockey has today almost entirely passed. But it may be said that horse-racing itself as a popular American sport has greatly declined. It has fallen into ill repute and under the heels of the reformers. Today not even the names of white jockeys are widely known. There were several factors in the passing of the Negro jockey, not the least of which was the economic one. When jockeys began to earn ten to twenty thousand dollars a year and even more, forces against the Negro were set in motion and kept at work until he was excluded. The same sort of thing might happen if the pay of Pullman porter's was raised to three hundred dollars a month.

The record of the Negro in professional baseball makes not so full a page. He did not have so much of a chance in baseball as he had in racing and pugilism. He never gets so fair a chance in those forms of sport or athletics where he must be a member of a team as in those where he may stand upon his own ability as an individual. The difficulty starts with prejudice against his becoming a team member. In baseball, as in racing, the Negro gained his first experience in the South. By 1880 nearly every city and town in the South had its coloured baseball club. For a period of years the best teams in the South were the coloured teams. For some reasons the whites were tardy about taking up the game and becoming proficient at it. In many places, however, they were fierce partisans and strong supporters of the black team of their town. Important match games between rival teams of different towns or states often drew as many white as black rooters and spectators. These were all amateur clubs, but several of them were as good as the professional clubs. Both Nashville and Memphis possessed crack coloured teams. Memphis had a wonderful pitcher named Higgins, and a catcher called "Peewee" Gwin, who was one of the first catchers in the game to take them off the bat. Nevertheless, in the middle eighties there were four coloured players on professional league teams. Rochester signed Higgins, formerly of the Memphis coloured team; Jersey City had a famous black battery, Stovey and Walker; and Buffalo had a star second baseman named Grant. Grant was dubbed "the Black Dunlap" after Dunlap of Detroit, who was then the most brilliant second baseman in the National League.

But the Negro player could not front the forces against him in organized baseball; so he was compelled to organize for himself. The first professional Negro team to be formed was the Gorhams of New York. From the Gorhams came the famous Cuban Giants. Following the success of the Cuban Giants, coloured professional and semi-professional clubs called Giants of some kind were organized in a dozen or more cities. These professional clubs have become better organized and now play a regularly scheduled series of games. They play very good ball and are quite popular, especially when they are pitted against white teams—and they are quite frequently in New York. The Cuban Giants were a remarkable aggregation and were widely known. The sports-writers gave them much space. They played fast ball and demonstrated it in games with league teams; but one of the main reasons why they were such good copy was the fact that they brought something entirely new to the professional diamond; they originated and introduced baseball comedy. The coaches kept up a constant banter that was spontaneous and amusing. They often staged a comic pantomime for the benefit of the spectators. When the team was in the field, the catcher habitually indulged in a continuous monologue in which he counselled and encouraged the pitcher or got off remarks not wholly complimentary to the batter. Generally after a good play the whole team would for a moment cut monkey-shines that would make the grand stand and bleachers roar. Delighted crowds went as much to hear as to see the Cuban Giants play ball. This style of baseball never gained much headway in the white professional clubs; most white players who tried it appeared foolish rather than funny. Arlie Latham of the old St. Louis Browns was a good comedian, and in more recent years the Washingtons have boasted a pair of splendid pantomimists; but, on the whole, baseball in the white professional world—at least, so far as the players were concerned—remained a dignified and rather grim performance. Nor has any other coloured club been the equal of the Cuban Giants in baseball comedy; and it is probable that the clubs of today do not wish to be quite their equals. Nevertheless, they all play the game in some degree after the manner of the first great Negro professional team.

The Negro's fairest chance in the professional sports came in the prize-ring. Here was brought into play more fully than in any other sport the advantageous factor of sole dependence upon his own individual skill and stamina. The prize-fighter had an advantage over even the jockey, who might be handicapped by hopeless mounts. The Negro prize-fighter, of course, often ran up against the hostility of the crowd, an intangible but, nevertheless, very real handicap. This very antagonism, however, according to the stout-heartedness of the fighter, might serve as a spur to victory. This is what actually happened when George Dixon defended his title of featherweight champion of the world and defeated Jack Skelly at New Orleans in 1892. This was more truly the case when Jack Johnson held his title of heavyweight champion of the world by knocking out Jim Jeffries at Reno, July 4, 1910. Johnson has said that not only did he have to fight Jeffries, but that psychologically he also had to fight the majority of the thousands of spectators, many of whom were howling and praying for Jeffries to "kill the nigger." In truth, Johnson had to do more; on that day he had to fight psychologically the majority of the population of the United States. Jeffries had been brought forth as "the hope of the white race." Indeed, during Johnson's term of championship and up to his defeat by Willard at Havana in 1915, every white fighter who was being groomed as a heavyweight contender was known as a "white hope." A good part of the press and some literary fellows were industrious in fomenting the sentiment that the security of white civilization and white supremacy depended upon the defeat of Jack Johnson. One of these writers assumed the role of both prophet and comforter and before the Reno battle wrote in the red-blooded style of the day that Jeffries was bound to win because, while he had Runnymede and Agincourt behind him, the Negro had nothing but the jungle; that the Negro would be licked the moment the white man looked him in the eye. This psychic manifestation of white superiority did not materialize, but that sort of thing did help to create a tenseness of feeling that constituted something real for Jack Johnson to contend with, and, furthermore, immediately after the fight, expended itself in the beating up of numerous individual Negroes in various parts of the country as a sort of vicarious obliteration of the blot of Jeffries's defeat, and in a manner not at all in accordance with the Marquis of Queensberry rules. In fact, the reaction was so great that pressure was brought which forced Congress to pass a law prohibiting the inter-state exhibition of moving pictures of prizefights—a law which still stands to plague and limit the magnates of pugilism and of the movies. Perhaps it was Jack Johnson's sense of humour almost as much as his skill and courage that enabled him to overcome this thing in the air. All through the fight he kept up a running banter with James J. Corbett, who was in Jeffries's comer. He would say to Corbett: "Watch this one, Jim. . . . How did you like that?" He relates that once in the midst of the fight he looked at Corbett's face and had to laugh. He says: "Jim's face reminded me of a man who had tasted his first green olive."

The story of the Negro in the prize-ring goes back much further than one would think; and, curiously, the beginning of the story is laid in New York City. The earliest acknowledgment of any man as champion of America was made about 1809; and that man was Thomas Molineaux (sometimes written Molyneaux). Tom Molineaux was born in 1784, a black slave belonging to a Molineaux (or Molyneaux) family of Virginia. When he was about twenty years old, he came to New York as a freeman and got a job as porter in the old Catherine Street market. The precise manner in which he procured his freedom does not seem to be known, but it appears that it was not by running away. Catherine market was headquarters for Negro boxers, and the new-comer soon proved himself the best of them all. It is more than probable that he did not reach New York a raw novice. There is a tradition that his father and grandfather before him had been boxers down in Virginia. For tradition also had it that boxing as a sport in this country began in Virginia; that in Virginia, more than in any other colony or state, it was the custom for the scions of aristocratic families to be sent to England as a part of their education, to rub shoulders with the gentry of the mother country and get the final polish that was deemed necessary for a Southern gentleman; that these young bloods witnessed prize-fights in England—where it was then and is now good form for the gentry not only to attend fights, but also to take lessons in the manly art—and brought the sport back home. Then, of course, the only way in which they could continue to enjoy it was to train likely young slaves as boxers and hold contests between the champions of different plantations. It can easily be imagined how much excitement and sport this would afford the rich planters.

Molineaux, after he had beaten every worthwhile fighter in America, both Negroes and the whites belonging to the crews of British vessels in port—white Americans had not yet taken up pugilism as a profession— was persuaded by the captain of one of the foreign vessels in port to go to England and seek a fight with the famed Tom Cribb, champion of England and of the world. He did go and, through the assistance of Bill Richmond, got the match. The fight between Cribb and Molineaux, which took place on December 18, 1810, at Capthall Common, Sussex, is one of the great prize-ring battles of England. Compared with the theatrical performances and businesslike transactions of today, it takes on titanic proportions. A reading of the contemporary accounts of the fight gives the impression of an ancient gladiatorial struggle to the death. The records of the time and later English authorities on boxing admit that, technically, Molineaux won the fight and consequently the championship of the world. He lost the decision through a bit of trickery on the part of Cribb's seconds. At the end of the twenty-eighth round both men were in such a condition that they had to be carried to their corners. When "Time!" was called for the twenty-ninth round Cribb was still so exhausted that he was unable to rise and respond. Joe Ward, in Cribb's corner, manoeuvred by immediately engaging Molineaux's seconds in a harangue on some point or other and thereby gained enough time to enable the champion to recover himself. The fight went on and was won by Cribb in the fortieth round. Molineaux at once issued another challenge, and a second fight for the championship of the world was fought on September 28, 1811. In this fight Molineaux was defeated. In that age, even as today, there were excuses or "alibis and it was asserted that Molineaux lost because up to the time of the fight he had to go barnstorming about the country in order to make a living, while Cribb underwent the best of training at Captain Barclay's estate in Scotland and was in the finest condition. It is to Molineaux's credit that this excuse was not offered by him. Molineaux fought and won a great many fights in England, Scotland, and Ireland. He lost two to Cribb, but the courage and stamina he displayed in both fights with the champion won for him the admiration of the fancy and the British public. He remains today one of the great figures in the history of the English prize-ring.

Bill Richmond, mentioned above, curiously, too, furnishes another thread that links this particular phase of our whole story to New York. When Molineaux reached England, he was taken under the patronage of Richmond, who was then one of the rulers in the English pugilistic world. And this same Richmond was a Negro, born a slave, on Staten Island, August 5, 1763. Pierce Egan, the noted contemporary historian of the English prize-ring, writing with no undue regard for syntax, says of Richmond:

When Sturton [Staten] Island was taken [held] by the English, young Richmond engaged the attention of General Earl Percy, the present Duke of Northumberland, who took him under his protection as his servant, and after traveling with the Earl abroad for some time, he arrived in England about the year 1777. The Duke, finding Bill to possess a good capacity and being an intelligent youth, had him put in school in Yorkshire, where he received a tolerably good education, and who afterwards apprenticed Richmond to the trade of cabinet maker and followed his business for a considerable time, not only in the above city but in the metropolis, as a journeyman, with credit to himself and respected by his employers.[2]

Richmond did not remain in the service of Earl Percy. Before he had long been in England, he attached himself to Lord Camelford, a sporting nobleman, and thence got into the prize-ring. He never fought in America, but fought and won a good many fights in England. He fought Cribb in 1805, five years before Molineaux fought the champion. This was the most amazing boxing-exhibition ever staged, up to that time. Richmond successfully carried out the plan of not allowing his opponent to hit him, and of not taking any chances in trying to hit his opponent. This dodge-and-run contest lasted an hour and a half and ended with the decision being awarded to Cribb. It should be said for Richmond that at the time of this fight he was forty-two years old and Cribb twenty-four. Yet in this

2. Quoted in Alexander Johnston: *Ten—and Out!* London, Chapman and Hall.

respect Richmond stands as the marvel of pugilism; age appears to have had little or no effect upon his ability to fight. After his fight with Cribb he retired from the ring and became the proprietor of a tavern, the Horse and Dolphin. He continued, however, to be active in the promotion of fights and often acted as a second. He was Cribb's second when the champion fought Jem Belcher. He prospered as a tavern-keeper and was regarded as a man of intelligence and standing. He became an intimate of the sportsmen of the nobility, among them Lord Byron. Then, as the marvel of pugilism, he came out from retirement in his fifty-second year and fought Davis, the navvy, who was then twenty-four years old, and defeated him in the thirteenth round by a knockout. The next year he fought Sailor Shelton, then twenty-eight years old, and knocked him out in the twenty-third round. At the finish of both these fights he leaped lightly over the ropes without a scratch on him. Nor was this the end. Two years later, when he was fifty-five years old, Richmond was one of a company of gentlemen having a pleasant evening "at a respectable tavern in the neighbourhood of Chancery Lane." Jack Carter, a successful fighter, known as the Lancashire Hero, intruded and made a nuisance of himself. The company rose and put him out. Carter, angered at this treatment, roared: "Is there a man among you dare face Jack Carter?" Richmond answered the challenge. An impromptu ring was cleared in the yard of the tavern. He knocked Carter out in three rounds. He died in 1829 highly respected by all who knew him. Molineaux died a charge upon his friends and charity.

Within the United States the Negro has made a high record in pugilism. In every important division of the sport since its organized establishment a Negro has held the championship of the world. In the bantamweight, George Dixon; featherweight, George Dixon; lightweight, Joe Gans; welterweight, Joe Walcott; middleweight, Tiger Flowers; light heavyweight, Battling Siki (won in France); heavyweight, Jack Johnson. In addition to these champions, there is a long list of notable Negro pugilists. There was George Godfrey of the old days in Boston. Then came Peter Jackson, who held the championship of Australia and against whom John L. Sullivan relentlessly drew the colour-line. Jackson is universally acknowledged as among the greatest of the great fighters. He fought Corbett sixty-one rounds to a draw in 1891. One year later he fought his famous battle with Frank Slavin before the National Sporting Club of London and defeated him. After that event his decline as a fighter set in. Peter Jackson was the first example in the United States of a man acting upon the assumption that he could be a prize-fighter and at the same time a cultured gentleman. His chivalry in the ring was so great that sports-writers down to today apply to him the doubtful compliment "a white coloured man." He was very popular in New York. If Jack Johnson had been in demeanour a Peter Jackson, the subsequent story of the Negro in the prize-ring would have been somewhat different. Nevertheless, it should be said for Johnson that, whatever he may have lacked in behaviour and good sense, he was a first-class fighting man, rated, in fact, the best defensive fighter the American ring has ever seen. During the first decade of the century there was a trio of formidable Negro heavyweights: Sam Langford, Sam McVey, and Joe Jeanette. One of the most sensational fighters in the ring today is Kid Chocolate (Eligio Sardinas), the black Cuban bantamweight.

New York, the New York of the upper Twenties and the lower Thirties, was the business and social centre of most of the coloured men engaged in these professional sports, as it was also of the genuine black-face minstrels, the forerunners of the later coloured performers; wherever their work might take them, they homed to New York. And because these men earned and spent large sums of money, there grew up in New York a flourishing black Bohemia.

EIGHT

NEW YORK'S BLACK BOHEMIA CONSTITUTED A part of the famous old Tenderloin; and, naturally, it nourished a number of the ever-present vices; chief among them, gambling and prostitution. But it nourished other things; and one of these things was artistic effort. It is in the growth of this artistic effort that we are here interested; the rest of the manifestations were commonplaces. This black Bohemia had its physical being in a number of clubs—a dozen or more of them well established and well known. There were gambling-clubs, honky-tonks, and professional clubs. The gambling-clubs need not be explained. The honky-tonks were places with paid and volunteer entertainers where both sexes met to drink, dance, and have a good time; they were the prototype of the modern night-club. The professional clubs were particularly the rendezvous of the professionals, their satellites and admirers. Several of these clubs were famous in their day and were frequented not only by blacks, but also by whites. Among the best-known were Joe Stewart's Criterion, the Douglass Club, the Anderson Club, the Waldorf, Johnny Johnson's, Ike Hines's, and later, and a little higher up, Barron Wilkins's Little Savoy, in West Thirty-fifth Street. The border line between the honky-tonks and some of the professional clubs was very thin. One of the latter that stood out as exclusively professional

was Ike Hines's. A description of a club—really Ike Hines's—is given in
The Autobiography of an Ex-Coloured Man.[1] That will furnish, perhaps,
a fresher picture of these places and the times than anything I might
now write:

> I have already stated that in the basement of the house there
> was a Chinese restaurant. The Chinaman who kept it did an
> exceptionally good business; for chop-suey was a favourite
> dish among the frequenters of the place.... On the main floor
> there were two large rooms: a parlour about thirty feet in
> length, and a large, square back room into which the parlour
> opened. The floor of the parlour was carpeted; small tables
> and chairs were arranged about the room; the windows were
> draped with lace curtains, and the walls were literally covered
> with photographs or lithographs of every coloured man in
> America who had ever 'done anything.' There were pictures
> of Frederick Douglass and of Peter Jackson, of all the lesser
> lights of the prize ring, of all the famous jockeys and the stage
> celebrities, down to the newest song and dance team. The
> most of these photographs were autographed and, in a sense,
> made a really valuable collection. In the back room there was
> a piano, and tables were placed round the wall. The floor was
> bare and the centre was left vacant for singers, dancers, and
> others who entertained the patrons. In a closet in this room
> which jutted out into the hall the proprietor kept his buffet.
>
> There was no open bar, because the place bad no liquor

---

1. James Weldon Johnson: *The Autobiography of an Ex-Coloured Man.* New
York, Alfred A. Knopf, 1927.

licence. In this back room the tables were sometimes pushed aside, and the floor given over to general dancing. The front room on the next floor was a sort of private party room; a back room on the same floor contained no furniture and was devoted to the use of new and ambitious performers. In this room song and dance teams practised their steps, acrobatic teams practised their tumbles, and many other kinds of 'acts' rehearsed their 'turns.' The other rooms of the house were used as sleeping-apartments.

No gambling was allowed, and the conduct of the place was surprisingly orderly. It was, in short, a centre of coloured Bohemians and sports. Here the great prizefighters were wont to come, the famous jockeys, the noted minstrels, whose names and faces were familiar on every billboard in the country; and these drew a multitude of those who love to dwell in the shadow of greatness. There were then no organizations giving performances of such order as are now given by several coloured companies; that was because no manager could imagine that audiences would pay to see Negro performers in any other role than that of Mississippi River roustabouts; but there was lots of talent and ambition. I often heard the younger and brighter men discussing the time when they would compel the public to recognize that they could do something more than grin and cut pigeon-wings.

Sometimes one or two of the visiting stage-professionals, after being sufficiently urged, would go into the back room and take the places of the regular amateur entertainers, but they were very sparing with their favours, and the patrons regarded them as special treats. There was one man, a minstrel, who, whenever he responded to a request to "do something," never essayed anything below a reading from Shakspere. How well he read I do not know, but he greatly impressed me; and I can say that at least he had a voice which strangely stirred those who heard it. Here was a man who made people laugh at the size of his mouth, while he carried in his heart a burning ambition to be a tragedian; and so after all he did play a part in a tragedy.

These notables of the ring, the turf, and the stage, drew to the place crowds of admirers, both white and coloured. Whenever one of them came in, there were awe-inspired whispers from those who knew him by sight, in which they enlightened those round them as to his identity, and hinted darkly at their great intimacy with the noted one. Those who were on terms of approach showed their privilege by gathering round their divinity. . . .

A great deal of money was spent here, so many of the patrons were men who earned large sums. I remember one night a dapper little brown-skin fellow was pointed out to me and I was told that he was the most popular jockey of the day, and that he earned $12,000 a year. This latter statement I couldn't doubt, for with my own eyes I saw him spending at about thirty times that rate. For his friends and those who were introduced to him he bought nothing but wine—in sporting circles, "wine" means champagne—and paid for it at five dollars a quart. . . . This jockey had won a great race that day, and he was rewarding his admirers for the homage they paid him, all of which he accepted with a fine air of condescension.

Besides the people I have just been describing, there were at the place almost every night one or two parties of white people, men and women, who were out sight-seeing, or slumming. They generally came in cabs; some of them would stay only for a few minutes, while others sometimes stayed until morning. There was also another set of white people that came frequently; it was made up of variety performers and others who delineated "darky characters they came to get their imitations first-hand from the Negro entertainers they saw there.

It was in such places as this that early Negro theatrical talent created for itself a congenial atmosphere, an atmosphere of emulation and guildship. It was also an atmosphere in which new artistic ideas were bom and developed. Early Negro theatrical talent, in so far as it was professional, belonged almost entirely to the minstrel stage. Antedating the minstrels, there were attempts made in the drama proper by Negro semi-professionals. As far back as 1821 the African Company gave performances of *Othello, Richard III*, and other classic plays, interspersed with comic acts, at the African Grove, corner of Bleecker and Mercer streets, "in the rear of the One Mile Stone, Broadway." The "One Mile Stone" refers to a stone which once stood at the corner of Broadway and Prince Street to mark the distance of one mile from City Hall. Later, the company becoming more prosperous or more ambitious, hired the "hotel" next door to the Grove for their performances. The New York *National Advocate* of October 27, 1821, in a facetious notice regarding their efforts, had this to say: "The gentlemen of color announce another play at their Pantheon, corner of Bleecker and Mercer Streets, on Monday evening. . . . They have graciously made a partition at the back of the house, for the accommodation of the whites."

The *National Advocate* also states that the attendance of whites out for a lark, and causing disorder, led to the closing of the theatre. But there is proof that it was reopened. Simon Snipe in a little book entitled *Sports of New York* describes a visit to the African Theatre which probably took place in the summer of 1823. He describes the theatre as well suited for warm weather, the breeze having free access through the crevices of the boards. He says that the orchestra consisted of a violin, a clarinet, and a bass fiddle, played by two white men and one black; that the audience was composed of "white, black, copper-coloured and light-brown." The play of the evening was *Othello*, and he reports it in the broadest burlesque manner. Laurence Hutton, in his *Curiosities of the American Stage*, reproduces a playbill of the African Company, dated June 7, the year not printed; but it is probable that the year was 1823. Conclusive proof that the African Company was giving performances at least as late as 1823 is furnished by a playbill cited by George C. D. Odell in *Annals of the New York Stage*. This bill announces performances for June 20 and 21, 1823, at the "theatre in Bleecker Street, in the rear of the One Mile Stone, Broadway," and states:

> "The Performers of the African Company have kindly united their services in order to contribute a Benefit to their Manager, Mr. Brown, who, for the first time, throws himself on the liberality of a generous public. Mr. Brown trusts that his unrelinquished exertions to please, will be justly considered by the Gentlemen and Ladies of this City, as on them depends his future support, and they can declare whether he is 'To be—or not to be—That is the question?'"[2]

2. George C. D. Odell: *Annals of the New York Stage,* III, 70. New York, Columbia University Press, 1928.

The prices of admission charged by the African Company are interesting in that they seem pretty high for the times and the patrons; the boxes were seventy-five cents, the pit fifty cents, and the gallery thirty-seven and a half cents. At the time of the benefit for Mr. Brown the prices had been or were lowered to fifty cents for box seats, and twenty-five cents for pit and gallery. In this later period the public is also called upon to "*Nota bene*: Proper officers will attend to keep order." In 1824 there was on Marion Street near Houston a place where dramatic plays were given by coloured performers. On March 30, 1826 James Hewlett, one of the original members of the African Company, gave a representation of "Shakespeare's proud heroes" at No. 11 Spruce Street. All of this early high-brow theatrical effort could be taken as pathetically ridiculous were it not that out of this same period sprang Ira Aldridge, one of the world's great tragedians.

There is great uncertainty about Aldridge's youth. The encyclopaedias all give varying accounts of his birth and his life before going on the stage. (The *Encyclopaedia Britannica* omits mention of Aldridge.) His birthplace is variously given as Belair, Maryland; Senegal, Africa; and New York City. The *Encyclopedia Americana* says of him:

"Aldridge, Ira Frederick, American negro tragedian: b. (?); d. Lodz, Poland, 7 Aug. 1867. The discrepancies about his birth and training are monstrous and indicate invention on one side. One is that he was a mulatto, born near Baltimore about 1810, who picked up German from immigrants, became Edmund Kean's servant, and developed stage talent under him in England, returned and made a theatrical failure in Baltimore 1830–31, then went back to England and became famous. The other is that he was the son of a full-blooded negro pastor in New York City (Greene Street Chapel), an immigrant Senegal chieftain converted and educated, who sent his son to Glasgow University to study for the same profession, despite a passion for the stage justified by successful amateur performances; but the boy (at this point the stories coincide) dropped theology and made his debut at the Royal Theatre as Othello. He took at once, and Kean made him Othello to his Iago in Belfast. He played Shakespearean roles in London till 1852, regarded as an excellent interpreter in all, but most liked in color-parts, such as Othello, Aaron in 'Titus Andronicus,' Rolla, Zanga, etc. He then played in Brussels and Germany 1852-55; the King of Sweden invited him to Stockholm in 1857. The Continent ranked him one of the foremost actors of the age, and the greatest sovereigns, with cities like Bern, showered honors and decorations on him and made him member of all sorts of learned societies. He married an Englishwoman. He was on his way to an engagement in Saint Petersburg when he died."

There is extant a still more extraordinary story about Aldridge's birth and youth; namely, that Daniel Aldridge, the father of Ira, was the son of a Senegalese king or chief who was brought to this country by missionaries; that three days after he left his native land, an insurrection broke out in which his father was overthrown and killed; that Daniel was educated and married in this country and remained here until he heard of the death of the usurper of his father's place, when he returned with his wife and attempted to regain his hereditary rights; that he met defeat and was obliged to stay in hiding for nine years, during which time Ira was born; that later he returned to America with the boy to carry out his plans to have him educated for the ministry. There are obvious reasons for doubting the accuracy of this story. There are also obvious reasons why Aldridge himself might not feel inclined to check its circulation or correct it. Such a story must have had a strong appeal to his dramatic imagination.

The accounts regarding his birth and early life differ, but, as the *Encyclopedia Americana* says, from the time of his leaving school the stories coincide. The writer has had the good fortune to see a photostat copy of one of Ira Aldridge's own scrap-books and from it has been able to construct what, in the main, is quite probably the true account of the tragedian's early years. From printed publicity material in the scrap-book, which, of course, came under the eyes of Aldridge himself, it appears that his father, known as Daniel Aldridge, was the son of a Senegalese chief and was brought to this country (perhaps first to Maryland) by missionaries to be educated so that he might go back to his people as a Christian ruler. He "was sent for his education to Schenectady College near New York in the United States." In the mean time his father was deposed and killed. Daniel, therefore, unable to return to his native land, became the pastor of a coloured church; according to this source of information, "a minister of the Presbyterian persuasion, and now officiates in Zion Chapel, New York." The immediately foregoing in formation is taken from a biographical note in a poster advertising Aldridge's appearance for ten performances at the Royal Adelphi Theatre, Hull, dated September 1, 1831. Daniel continued as a preacher in New York until he died, September 27, 1840, "greatly regretted by his coloured brethren."

Ira was born July 24, 1807. It is probable that New York City was the place of his birth, and that it was there his education was begun. Henry Highland Garnett's address delivered in the House of Representatives was published, together with a sketch of his life written by Dr. James McCune Smith, a contemporary and a very prominent New York Negro. The sketch states that Garnett was first a pupil of African Free School No. 1 in New York and mentions as others who had attended the same school and risen to distinction in life: Patrick Reason, the engraver; Samuel Ringgold Ward, the orator; Alexander Crummell, the preacher; and Ira Aldridge, the actor. Dr. Smith, though younger, was of Aldridge's generation and may, as a boy, have seen and known him.

It also appears that while but a boy Aldridge made his first appearance on the stage in the character of Rolla, the hero in Sheridan's *Pizarro*, with an "all Negro cast at a private theatre." This performance, it is most probable, took place in New York City. He got employment of some sort—it may have been as call-boy—which took him behind the scenes at the Chatham Theatre, where he listened nightly to the actors declaiming their lines. It was with great reluctance that he left this work, which fascinated him to go on with his education. It is possible that Aldridge, before he was sent to Glasgow, attended for a while the same school to which his father had gone. It seems that he was at Glasgow about a year and a half, but in that time made something of a record for scholarship, winning several prizes and the medal for Latin composition. He then abandoned his studies and went to London, where, after considerable difficulty, he made an appearance as Othello at the Royalty, an East End theatre. He made a favourable impression, and from that time on, his climb to success was steady. From the Royalty he went to the Coburg and gave performances of *Oroonoko* and other plays. While he was playing at the Coburg, there came a young lady, a member of a private box party, to see his performance. She shortly afterwards became his wife. He went from the Coburg to Sadler's Wells Theatre. He then decided to leave London and go through the study and practice which "he deemed necessary for a sound metropolitan reputation." He made an extended tour of the provinces, "playing Brighton, Chichester, Leicester, Liverpool, Manchester, Glasgow, Edinburg, Exeter, and other towns." He opened at Covent Garden in *Othello*, April 10, 1833.[3]

For a long time he was unable to get an engagement in Dublin because the manager of the theatre could not be induced to engage a Negro actor. Aldridge went to Dublin and had a personal interview with the manager, Mr. Calcraft, and obtained an engagement for a limited period. He opened in *Othello* and was a sensation. It was during this engagement that Edmund Kean saw his performance, and the result was Kean's Iago to Aldridge's Othello, and an intimate friendship between the two men. Othello was his favourite and most famous role. By playing the role of Aaron, the Moor, in *Titus Andronicus*, he restored to the English stage a play which, prior to 1851, had not been acted for two centuries. The accounts of his professional appearances in the United States are too fragmentary to afford any definite information. Indeed, it seems doubtful that he ever did so appear. In one of the posters in the scrap-book Messrs. Ingleton and Clifton, announcing his engagement for their theatre, refer to "his successes in New York and the principal theaters of the United States." Most likely this is a reference, exaggerated for publicity purposes, to his successes as a youthful amateur.

3. *London Opinion* was led to comment upon Ira Aldridge in its issue of March 13, 1915, the occasion being the death of his widow, a second wife, the former Countess Amanda Pauline Brandt, at the age of eighty-two. It is there stated that his first appearance in London was with the company of the Victoria Theatre in Waterloo Road.

Aldridge had large success in Great Britain, but it was on the Continent that he was first accorded unqualified recognition; it was on the Continent that he was most enthusiastically acclaimed. There is a story that one night after his performance of Othello in Saint Petersburg the students unhitched the horses from his carriage and themselves drew it back to his hotel. He was an intimate friend of Alexandre Dumas. In the correspondence between Richard Wagner and Mathilde Wesendonck there appears the following note from him to her: "Take notice:—Wednesday: *Othello*—Ira Aldridge. Tickets should be booked in time. The top of the morning. R. W."

In 1865, the Chevalier Ira Aldridge made his last professional visit to London; it was during this visit that the Desdemona to his Othello at the Haymarket was Mrs. Kendal. This was at the beginning of Mrs. Kendal's great career; and of the engagement she herself wrote:

> During the time that I was there, Mr. Ira Aldridge was engaged to act. Mr. Ira Aldridge was a man who, being black, always picked out the fairest woman he could to play Desdemona with him, not because she was capable of acting the part, but because she had a fair head. One of the great bits of "business" that he used to do was where in one of the scenes he had to say: "Your hand, Desdemona." He made a very great point of opening his hand and making you place yours in it, and the audience used to see the contrast.
>
> He always made a point of it and got a round of applause; how, I do not know. It always struck me that he had some species of—well, I will not say "genius," because I dislike that word as used nowadays—but gleams of great intelligence. Although a genuine black, he was quite *preux chevalier* in his

manners to women.

Just before his death Aldridge had about completed arrangements for an American tour. He died in Lodz, Poland, and was given a civic funeral.

In December 1928, at the request of the committees organized for the purpose of rebuilding the Shakespeare Memorial Theatre at Stratford-on-Avon, I undertook to plan the raising of one thousand dollars by coloured people in the United States for the endowment of an Ira Aldridge Memorial Chair in the theatre. A committee was formed and the money promptly raised and forwarded through the American Shakespeare Foundation to the Shakespeare Memorial Fund in England.

But Ira Aldridge was a sport; his career was in no degree a direct factor in the Negro's theatrical development. In a less degree did the efforts made at the African Grove Theatre have any consequent effects. The real beginnings of the Negro in the American theatre were made on the minstrel stage. Negro minstrelsy, as a popular form of professional entertainment, seems dead; nevertheless, its history cannot be reviewed without recognition of the fact that it was the first and remains, up to this time, the only completely original contribution America has made to the theatre. Negro minstrelsy, everyone ought to know, had its origin among the slaves of the old South. Every plantation had its talented band that could crack Negro jokes, and sing and dance to the accompaniment of the banjo and the bones—the bones being the actual ribs of a sheep or some other small animal, cut the proper length and scraped clean and bleached in the sun. When the wealthy plantation-owner wished to entertain and amuse his guests, he needed only to call for his troupe of black minstrels. There is a record of at least one of these bands that became semi-professional and travelled round from plantation to plantation giving performances.

White actors very early realized the commercial value of Negro impersonation and as far back as the beginning of the nineteenth century began putting on single black-face acts. The most famous of these "singles" was Dan Rice's "Jump Jim Crow." In the summer of 1830, according to an account in the *Atlantic Monthly* of November 1867, Rice, then an obscure performer, was sauntering through the streets of Cincinnati when he heard a ragged Negro singing the "Jump Jim Crow" song. The idea at once struck him that with the song and the impersonation he could make a hit. He put the act on in the fall at Pittsburgh and did make a hit. Indeed, "Jump Jim Crow" made Dan Rice famous. Later, during an engagement in Washington, Rice made the act a "double," his partner being Joseph Jefferson, then about four years old. Rice brought him on in a sack slung over his shoulder and, stepping down to the footlights, sang:

> "Ladies and gentlemen, I'd have you for to know
> That I've got a little darky here that jumps Jim Crow";

with which he emptied little Jefferson from the sack, made up, rags, black face, and all, as a diminutive and imitating counterpart. This was Joseph Jefferson's debut on the stage.

The first black-face minstrel troupe to give a worked-up performance in a regular theatre was a quartet of white men headed by Dan Emmett, the man who wrote "Dixie"; they called themselves the Virginia Minstrels, and opened in New York City during the first part of February 1843. Almost simultaneously troupes sprang up in the larger Northern cities, and Negro minstrelsy was at once on its way to the great popularity it was to hold for more than sixty years. These troupes took such names as: Virginia Serenaders, Ethiopian Minstrels, and Kentucky Minstrels. Later troupes bore the names of their organizers or managers. Minstrelsy flourished and it was developed and elaborated to such a degree that it became less and less an imitation of Negro plantation life, and towards the end of the last century it provided the most gorgeous stage spectacle to be seen in the United States. All of these companies did not remain entirely white; the most notable exception was the troupe taken out by Primrose and West in 1893, known as "The Forty Whites and Thirty Blacks."

The full entry of the Negro himself upon the professional minstrel stage took place towards the end of the sixties, although Lew Johnson's Plantation Minstrel Company was organized during the early part of the decade. These troupes composed of Negroes accepted almost wholly the performance pattern as it had been worked out and laid down by the white minstrels during the preceding twenty-five years, even to blacking their faces, an expedient which, of course, never entered the minds of the original plantation artists. However, these performers could not help bringing to professional minstrelsy something fresh and original. They brought a great deal that was new in dancing, by exhibiting in their perfection the jig, the buck and wing, and the tantalizing stop-time dances. Billy Kersands, the most famous of all the genuine Negro minstrels, introduced the Virginia "essence," which constituted one of the fundamental steps in Negro dancing. One of the specialties of the two Bohee brothers was a soft-shoe dance in the calcium light while they sang and accompanied themselves on their banjos. And it appears that the creator of the minstrel and vaudeville monologue was Charles Cruso, a Negro minstrel of the early seventies who was billed as "The Man Who Talks." Wallace King and Billy Windom, two of the most famous of minstrel tenors, did a great deal to give a certain style of singing popularity. King made clever use of falsetto, as did Windom, who was billed as "the singer with the child voice."

The first successful all-Negro company was the Georgia Minstrels, organized in 1865 by Charles Hicks, a Negro. Hicks found the hostility to doing business with a coloured manager too great a handicap; so, after two or three seasons of ups and downs, the management was taken over by Charles Callender, and the company became known as Callender's Original Georgia Minstrels. It was headed by Billy Kersands. A little later, Sam Lucas was added to the list. Sam Lucas came to be the Grand Old Man of the Negro stage. He was born in Washington, Ohio, in 1840, was well educated, cultured in his manners, and a neat dresser. He was the sort of man that looks well in a frock-coat. He was a versatile performer and was active on the stage from those early days of minstrelsy down to modern Negro musical comedy. As late as 1910 he played a leading part in Cole and Johnson's *Red Moon*. In 1915 he played the role of Uncle Tom in the first screen version of *Uncle Tom's Cabin*, himself making the plunge into the river to save Little Eva. His friends felt that this feature of his performance helped to bring on his fatal illness. He died in New York January 10, 1916. In addition to these qualities Sam Lucas possessed another valuable attribute as an actor, especially for those times. Daniel Frohman and Isaac Marcosson in their *Life of Charles Frohman* relate that Gustave Frohman started as advance-agent with the Callender Ministrels in August 1872; that later he became manager of the show and secured the place of advance-agent for his brother Daniel; that at the close of 1876 Gustave Frohman quit the Callender Ministrels and he and George Stoddart launched the Stoddart Comedy Company, with John Dillon as star. He gave his brother Charles the job of advance-agent. The show played in terrible luck and was several times on the verge of stranding, in spite of the heroic efforts of the youthful and enthusiastic Charles. The company, by hook or by crook, worked its way up through Texas, Arkansas, and Tennessee to Richmond, Kentucky. The biographers of Mr. Frohman then go on to say:

> At Richmond Gustave had an inspiration. Then, as always, "Uncle Tom's Cabin" was the great life-saver of the harassed and needy theatrical organization. . . .
>
> "Why not have a real negro play Uncle Tom?" said Gustave.
>
> So he wired Charles as follows:
>
> *"Get me an Eva and send her down with Sam Lucas. Be sure to tell Sam to bring his diamonds."*
>
> Sam Lucas was a famous negro minstrel who had been with the Callender company. He sported a collection of diamonds that made him the envy and admiration of his colleagues. Gustave knew that these jewels, like Louise Dillon's sealskin sack, meant a meal ticket for the company and transportation in an emergency.
>
> Charles engaged Sallie Cohen (now Mrs. John C. Rice), and sent her down with Lucas, who, by the way, provided the money for the trip.

Gustave Frohman had visions of big business in Ohio, but *Uncle Tom* couldn't save them, and Wilmington, Ohio, "proved to be the last despairing gasp of the Stoddart Comedy Company, for the trouble-studded tour now ended. Some of Lucas's diamonds were pawned to get the company back to Cincinnati."

In 1878 Jack Haverly bought the Callender Minstrels. Gustave Frohman was again the manager for a while and took the troupe on a tour to the Pacific coast. The Callender company, two or three years later, went to Europe under the name of Haverly's European Minstrels. In the company were: Billy Kersands, Sam Lucas, James Bland, Billy Speed, Irving Sayles, Tom McIntosh, and the Bohee brothers. The three Frohmans had in the mean time taken over the Madison Square Theatre in New York, but Gustave Frohman conceived the plan of getting together the largest Negro minstrel company ever organized and making a grand tour of the United States. In June 1882 he sent his brother Charles to England to get, if possible, the pick of Haverly's Europeans, then playing there. Charles Frohman accomplished his errand by purchasing the whole company from Haverly and bringing it back to the United States. There was then put on the road Callender's Consolidated Spectacular Colored Minstrels. On all the bills appeared the inscription "Gustave and Charles Frohman, Proprietors." Charles Frohman brought back the whole company with the exception of the Bohee brothers and one or two others. The two Bohee brothers were, perhaps, the first finished performers on the banjo. They were very popular, especially in England, and one of them, James, never came back. They were successful both as performers and as teachers. James Bohee was instructor on the banjo to the then Prince of Wales.

In the palmy days of minstrelsy, the eighties and nineties, besides several lessee troupes, there were three large, well-known Negro companies that bore the names of their coloured managers and owners. These were: the Hicks and Sawyer Minstrels (the same Hicks as he of the Georgia Minstrels), the Richards and Pringle Minstrels, and the McCabe and Young Minstrels.

Minstrelsy was, on the whole, a caricature of Negro life, and it fixed a stage tradition which has not yet been entirely broken. It fixed the tradition of the Negro as only an irresponsible, happy-go-lucky, wide-grinning, loud-laughing, shuffling, banjo-playing, singing, dancing sort of being. Nevertheless, these companies did provide stage training and theatrical experience for a large number of coloured men. They provided an essential training and theatrical experience which, at the time, could not have been acquired from any other source. Many of these men, as the vogue of minstrelsy waned, passed on into the second phase, or middle period, of the Negro on the theatrical stage in America; and it was mainly upon the training they had gained that this second phase rested.

NINE

PRECEDING AND DURING THE SECOND PERIOD in the Negro's theatrical development there were a number of what might be termed semi-professional companies that went from town to town, making their own engagements and hiring theatres, halls, or churches for their performances. These efforts were generally of an ambitious character. Of these small troupes the best were those whose programs were mostly musical. The musical troupes actually antedated the minstrels, and the best of them was one of the very earliest, the Luca family. This troupe originally consisted of six members, father, mother, and four sons, all of them highly talented. The father was bom in Milford, Connecticut, and the sons were born and reared in New Haven. The Luca family gained its first wide public recognition in singing at the anniversary of the Anti- Slavery Society held in the old Broadway Tabernacle in 1853. Accounts of their appearance record "the wildest enthusiasm." The company travelled through the Northern and Western states and gained a high reputation. But in the professional theatre the first successful departure made by the Negro from strict minstrelsy was in 1890. Sam T. Jack, a prominent burlesque-theatre owner and manager, conceived the idea of putting out a Negro show different from anything yet thought of, a show that would glorify the coloured girl. He got together some clever men, among them Sam Lucas, Fred Piper, Billy Jackson, and Irving Jones, and a chorus of the sixteen most beautiful coloured girls he could secure, and opened the *Creole Show*. The *Creole Show* gave great prominence to girls and was smart and up-to-date in material and costumes. It had none of the features of plantation days; nevertheless, it was cast in the traditional minstrel pattern. There was a minstrel first part, differing, however, from the regular minstrel show in that the girls were in the centre of the line, with a female interlocutor, and the men on the ends; then came an olio, and then the finale. Notwithstanding, it was the start along a line which led straight to the musical comedies of Cole and Johnson, Williams and Walker, and Ernest Hogan. The important performers were assembled in New York; the company rehearsed at Haverhill, Massachusetts, and the show had its real opening at the Howard in Boston. The Creoles opened in Chicago in 1891; during the whole season of the World's Fair, 1893, they played at Sam T. Jack's Opera House in that city. They created something of a sensation in New York when they edged up to the "Broadway zone" by playing at the old Standard Theatre in Greeley Square. *The Creole Show* ran for five or six seasons. A year or so after the organization of the Creoles, Whallen and Martell, two white managers, brought up from Louisville, Kentucky, a show called *South Before the War*. This was an entertainment made up of plantation scenes, songs, and dances, with some specialties. It was popular in the burlesque houses and played for several seasons.

In 1895 John W. Isham, who had been the advance-agent of the *Creole Show*, went out for himself and produced *The Octoroons*. This company was organized in New York; and following it every important Negro theatrical production has been organized there. *The Octoroons* was a step further along than the *Creole Show*, but it also adhered in a general way to the minstrel pattern. It was billed, "a Musical Farce," but it was made up of a first part, a middle part, and a finale, neither one having any sequential connexion with the others. The first part consisted of an opening chorus and a medley of songs done by the various principals, generally assisted by the girls of the chorus. The middle part was a burlesque sketch in which a number of specialties were strung on a very thin thread of story. The show closed with a cake-walk jubilee, a military drill, and a "chorus-march-finale." The synopsis declared all the scenes to be laid in New York City. Like the *Creole Show*, *The Octoroons* made a special feature of the girls, but not only as chorus members; a half-dozen of them were used as principals. *The Octoroons*, as did both its predecessors, played the burlesque houses.

In 1896 Mr. Isham produced *Oriental America*. This was a more ambitious production than *The Octoroons*; for although it was built on the minstrel model, the afterpiece, instead of being made up of burlesque and specialties, cake-walk, "hoe-down," and walk-around finale, was a medley of operatic selections. Mr. Isham, in addition to having in the company clever performers and pretty girls, had some of the best-trained Negro singers available. He signed Sidney Woodward, who had quite a reputation in Boston as a tenor; J. Rosamond Johnson, then a student of music in the same city; William C. Elkins, Miss Maggie Scott, and several others who had made a study of singing. Miss Inez Clough, who, more recently, has achieved success in Negro dramatic plays, was also a member of the company. The finale of the show consisted of solos and choruses from *Faust*, *Martha*, *Rigoletto*, *Carmen*, and *Il Trovatore*. *Oriental America* broke all precedents by being the first coloured show to play Broadway proper; it opened at Wallack's Theatre, at that time called Palmer's. *Oriental America* broke further away from the minstrel patterns than did the *Creole Show* and *The Octoroons,* and it was the first coloured show to make a definite break from the burlesque houses.

In the mean time Worth's Museum, at Sixth Avenue and Thirtieth Street, had virtually become a Negro stock theatre, the first place where a group of coloured performers were able to gain anything approaching dramatic training and experience on the strictly professional stage. The company was composed of twelve to fifteen performers, both men and women, and was for a period headed by Bob Cole, who had been a member of the *Creole Show.* He was both playwright and stage-manager and provided a series of sketches and plays that made Worth's Museum All-Star Stock Company very popular. At this time Bob Cole was about twenty-six years old, but he was already evincing the powers which were to make him the greatest single force in the middle period of the development of the Negro in the American theatre. He was the most versatile theatrical man the Negro has yet produced: a good singer and an excellent dancer, and able to play several musical instruments. He could write a dramatic or a musical play—dialogue, lyrics, and music—stage the play, and act a part. In his role as a tramp he received the highest praise of the critics. Moreover, he was educated and a serious student of the whole history of the theatre and the drama.

And now a slight digression. Beginning quite early, coloured singers made considerable headway on the concert stage. Contrary to what holds true at the present time, the most successful of them were women. As far back as 1851, Elizabeth Taylor Greenfield, known as the "Black Swan," attracted attention by singing for the Buffalo (New York) Musical Association. She followed this appearance with concerts before discriminating audiences in the larger cities and towns upstate in New York, and through New England and the Middle Western states. She then decided to visit Europe. Thereupon the citizens of Buffalo tendered her a benefit concert, which took place on March 7, 1853. A few weeks later she appeared in a successful concert before a very large audience in New York City; and on April 6 she sailed for England. She made an astonishing impression on the English public, and on May 4, 1854 she was "commanded to attend at Buckingham Palace" and sing before Queen Victoria. The "Black Swan" died in Philadelphia in 1876. Just about the time of her death the Hyers sisters, Anna Madah and Emma Louise, were at the top of their popularity. These two sisters, one a soprano and the other a contralto, gave concerts in which they were well received throughout all the Northern and Western states. Then came the first coloured singer with both the natural voice and the necessary training and cultivation, Mme Marie Selika. Mme Selika studied under good teachers in the United States and in Europe, becoming proficient in German and French, especially German, which she made her second language. She sang with success in this country and abroad. She is at present a teacher of singing in the Martin-Smith School of Music in Harlem. Several others gained notice also, among them Flora Batson, who possessed an almost unnatural range and was a marvellous singer of ballads.

But the most popular of all these women singers was Sissieretta Jones, known as the "Black Patti." The height of her career was so recent that her name and fame will be recalled by a great many who read these lines. She had most of the qualities essential in a great singer: the natural voice, the physical figure, the grand air, and the engaging personality. Sissieretta Jones had studied and been singing in concert for several years, but first gained wide publicity by her singing at a Jubilee Spectacle and Cake-Walk which was staged at Madison Square Garden April 26–8, 1892, for which she had been specially engaged. She sang three nights and carried off the honours of the affair. The next day the New York papers gave her space and headlines, and by one critic she was dubbed "Black Patti." Her manager was emboldened to take her to the Academy of Music, which had been dark all the week, and she sang there to large audiences for two nights immediately after the close of the Jubilee. So great was the sensation she created that there was talk of having her sing the dark roles in *Aida* and *La Africaine* at the Metropolitan Opera House. In fact, she was signed by Abbey, Schoffel, and Grau, then managers of the Metropolitan, but the plans for grand opera were not carried out, and she was booked on the concert stage. Later she came under the management of Major Pond. In September 1892 she was invited by President Harrison to sing at a White House reception. Later in the same month she was engaged to sing for a week at the Pittsburgh Exposition as soloist with Levy's Band. That season she toured the country as soloist with the band. The following year she was engaged again to sing at the Pittsburgh Exposition, this time as soloist with Gilmore's Band. She then made a concert tour of Europe, which lasted nearly a year.

When "Black Patti" returned, she came under the management of Voelckel and Nolan of New York, who carried out their plan of taking Sissieretta Jones off the concert stage and presenting her in an all-Negro show. They engaged Bob Cole to write it; and in the same season with *Oriental America*, "Black Patti's Troubadours" was produced. "Black Patti's Troubadours," too, in a general way followed the minstrel pattern. The first part was a sketchy farce interspersed with songs and choruses and ending with a buck-dance contest. Then followed an olio. The finale was termed: "The Operatic Kaleidoscope," and in it "Black Patti" appeared in songs and operatic selections with the chorus. She took no other part in the show, but was the great drawing card. The Troubadours played season after season for a number of years. One reason for the long life of the show was "Black Patti's" great popularity in the South. The Troubadours, alone among the larger coloured shows, was able to play successfully in the South. Sissieretta Jones has retired from both the theatrical and the concert stage and lives at her home in Providence, Rhode Island.

During the first season of the Troubadours, while the company was playing at Proctor's Fifty-eighth Street Theatre in New York, Bob Cole had a serious disagreement with Messrs. Voelckel and Nolan regarding salary. Not reaching a satisfactory agreement, he gathered up the music that he had written and walked out with it. This action led to his arrest, and he was haled into court. Before the magistrate he declared: "These men have amassed a fortune from the product of my brain, and now they call me a thief; I won't give it up!" However, as is usual, the stronger side won. But the rupture between Bob Cole and the managers of the Troubadours marked an epoch in Negro theatricals, for he began at once to plan a play of his own. In the season of 1898–9 he came out with *A Trip to Coontown*, the first Negro show to make a complete break from the minstrel pattern, the first that was not a mere potpourri, the first to be written with continuity and to have a cast of characters working out the story of a plot from beginning to end; and, therefore, the first Negro musical comedy. It was, furthermore, the first coloured show to be organized, produced, and managed by Negroes. Some of the best performers then on the stage united with Cole in *A Trip to Coontown*; among them Billy Johnson, who became Cole's partner and was the Johnson of the first Cole and Johnson combination; Sam Lucas, and Jesse Shipp, who later was the directing genius in the construction of the Williams and Walker plays. *A Trip to Coontown* ran three seasons.

The summer of 1898 marked another great step forward. Will

Marion Cook composed the music to a sketch entitled *Clorindy—The Origin of the Cake-Walk*, with lyrics by Paul Laurence Dunbar. The play was produced by George W. Lederer at the Casino Roof Garden and ran the entire summer season. The cast included Ernest Hogan, a veteran minstrel and a very funny, natural-black-face comedian; and Miss Belle Davis, who later made a success in Europe and stayed there. Hogan was a notable exception among black-face comedians; his comic effects did not depend upon the caricature created by the use of cork and a mouth exaggerated by paint. His mobile face was capable of laughter-provoking expressions that were irresistible, notwithstanding the fact that he was a very good-looking man. Some critics ranked him higher than Bert Williams. He had greater unction than Bert Williams and by that very token lacked Williams's subtlety and finish. *Clorindy* was the talk of New York. It was the first demonstration of the possibilities of syncopated Negro music. Cook was the first competent composer to take what was then known as rag-time and work it out in a musicianly way. His choruses and finales in *Clorindy*, complete novelties as they were, sung by a lusty chorus, were simply breath-taking. Broadway had something entirely new.

The following summer another musical playlet, *Jes Lak White Folks*, written by Cook, was produced at the New York Winter Garden. In this playlet Cook was less fortunate in his sketch material and in his cast; Hogan had gone to the Antipodes at the head of the Senegambians under the management of M. B. Curtis of "Sam'l of Posen" fame. Curtis skipped and left the company stranded in Australia. *Jes Lak White Folks* had among its principals a girl named Abbie Mitchell, who was later to be important in Negro Musical comedy and dramatics. Irving Jones was the comedian. Will Marion Cook continued to develop his distinctive style in composing the music for the later shows of Williams and Walker.

TEN

WILLIAMS AND WALKER CAME FROM OUT of the West. They came singing one of the catchiest songs of the day, "Dora Dean," which they themselves had written after the quite adequate inspiration of a sight of Miss Dora Dean, one of the famed beauties of the *Creole Show*. They reached New York in 1896. They had been together as a team for several years, undergoing all the special vicissitudes of a coloured vaudeville team of the period, when they were engaged to appear in *The Gold Bug*, produced at the Casino Theatre by Canary and Lederer. *The Gold Bug* did not quite catch Broadway's fancy, but Williams and Walker did; and after the failure of the Casino show they were engaged for the famous Koster and Bial's, where they played a record run of forty weeks. It was during this engagement that Williams and Walker made the cake-walk not only popular, but fashionable. They were assisted by two girls; one of them, Stella Wiley, was the cleverest coloured soubrette of the day. Cake-walk pictures posed for by the quartet were reproduced in colours and widely distributed as advertisements by one of the big cigarette concerns. And the execution of cake-walk steps was taken up by society. Cake-walking became such a society fad that on Sunday morning, January 16, 1898, Williams and Walker, dressed just a point or two above the height of fashion, dared, as a publicity stunt, to call at the home of William K. Vanderbilt and leave the following letter:

To Mr. William K. Vanderbilt
Comer of Fifty-second Street and Fifth Avenue
New York
Dear Sir:

In view of the fact that you have made a success as a cake-walker, having appeared in a semi-public exhibition and having posed as an expert in that capacity, we, the undersigned world-renowned cake-walkers, believing that the attention of the public has been distracted from us on account of the tremendous hit which you have made, hereby challenge you to compete with us in a cake-walking match, which will decide which of us shall deserve the title of champion cake-walker of the world.

As a guarantee of good faith we have this day deposited at the office of the New York *World* the sum of $50. If you purpose proving to the public that you really are an expert cake-walker we shall be pleased to have you cover that amount and name the day on which it will be convenient for you to try odds against us.

Yours very truly,
Williams and Walker.

Regarding the size of the stakes, Williams, who habitually left all business matters to Walker, is reported as saying: "It's a shame to take the money, so make the stakes small, George."

The two comedians next tried the London music halls, but the

English appeared not to be able to understand or appreciate their particular brand of humour; so they came back to New York and went out at the head of a mediocre show, A Senegambian Carnival, which promptly stranded. They followed with 4–11–44, afterwards changed to The Policy Players. This was also a failure. In 1900 they brought out The Sons of Ham, and in this humorous-pathetic musical farce they struck their stride. In 1902 they produced In Dahomey and made Negro theatrical history by opening at the very centre of theatredom, at the New York Theatre in Times Square. In the spring of 1903 In Dahomey was taken to London. The two principals, remembering their reception in the London music-halls, were somewhat apprehensive about the venture; but the show was a success and ran for seven months at the Shaftesbury Theatre, afterwards touring the provinces. The unquestioned stamp of approval was put on it when at the end of the first month the company received a royal command for a performance at Buckingham Palace, on June 23. The performance was part of the celebration in honour of the ninth birthday of the present Prince of Wales and was given on a stage erected on the lawn. In Dahomey made the cake-walk a social fad in England and France. In 1906 Williams and Walker opened with In Abyssinia at the Majestic Theatre in Columbus Circle, New York. This was followed by Bandana Land in 1907.

Bandana Land was the last play in which Williams and Walker appeared together; during its run George Walker's health broke and he never again stepped on the stage. The Williams and Walker company was, all in all, the strongest Negro theatrical combination that has yet been assembled. In addition to Williams and Walker there were Jesse Shipp, Alex Rogers, Will Marion Cook, and Ada Overton. Mr. Shipp had had long theatrical experience, beginning with minstrelsy, and he it was who worked out the details of the construction of the plays, after the idea had been discussed and adopted by the above-named heads. Mr. Rogers was the lyricist and the author of the words to many of the most popular of the Williams and Walker songs; among them: "Why Adam Sinned," "I May Be Crazy, but I Ain't No Fool," "The Jonah Man," "Bon Bon Buddy, the Chocolate Drop," and "Nobody." He also contributed much of the droll humour and many of the ludicrous situations for which these plays were noted. Mr. Cook, of whom we have already spoken, was the composer-in-chief. Ada Overton (Mrs. George Walker) was beyond comparison the brightest star among women on the Negro stage of the period; and it is a question whether or not she has since been surpassed. She was an attraction in the company not many degrees less than the two principals. And there was also one of the best singing choruses ever heard on a musical-comedy stage. Of course the main strength of the combination centred in the two comedians; George Walker as the sleek, smiling, prancing dandy, and Bert Williams as the slow-witted, good-natured, shuffling darky. Together they achieved something beyond mere fun; they often achieved the truest comedy through the ability they had to keep the tears close up under the loudest laughter.

Bert Williams went out alone in 1909 in *Mr. Lode of Kole*, which had little success and was the last Negro show in which he ever appeared. The next year he was engaged for the Ziegfeld *Follies* and remained a member of the cast for practically ten seasons. In 1920 he was the star in *Broadway Brevities,* and in 1922 the star in *The Pink Slip*, which after a tryout was rewritten and called *Under the Bamboo Tree.* He was a sick man when he went out with this last play; and after it had been on the road but a few weeks, he had to be brought back to New York. He died March 11, 1922, not yet forty-seven years old. Bert Williams goes down as one of America's great comedians. He has had few equals in the art of pantomime—a judgment with which those who saw him in his poker scene will agree. In the singing of a plaintive Negro song he was beyond approach. His singing of "Nobody" was perfection.

After three seasons with Cole and Johnson's *A Trip to Coontown* Bob Cole, in 1901, formed a partnership with another Johnson, this time J. Rosamond Johnson, the musician and singer, and the new Cole and Johnson became head-liners in big-time vaudeville. They sang their own songs and were a success in this country and in Europe. In the mean time they collaborated on the writing of white musical plays, and through this some of their songs gained worldwide popularity. In 1906 Cole and Johnson wrote and appeared in a musical play called *The Shoofly Regiment*, which played in New York at the Bijou Theatre on Broadway. In 1908 they came out in another play of their own, *The Red Moon*. Each of these plays was a true operetta with a well-constructed book and a tuneful, well-written score. On these two points no Negro musical play has equalled *The Red Moon*. The Cole and Johnson combination lacked any such fun-makers as were Williams and Walker, but in some other respects they excelled their great rivals; their plays, on the whole, were better written, and they carried a younger, sprightlier, and prettier chorus, which, though it could not sing so powerfully, could outdance the heavier chorus of the other company by a wide margin.

The break in health that ended the careers of Bob Cole and George Walker, and the defection of Bert Williams to the white stage, all happening within a brief period of time, put a sudden stop to what had been a steady development and climb of the Negro in the theatre. In this first decade of the century plays headed by Ernest Hogan and Smart and Williams, and S. H. Dudley, and some other performers, were produced, but all these shows, though organized in New York, were road shows and of secondary merit. The Hogan shows, *Rufus*

Rastus and *The Oyster Man*, were the most important of them. Hogan might have carried on, because he was a splendid comedian and had a New York reputation; but he died a short while before George Walker's retirement.

There came an interval, and the efforts of the Negro in New York in the theatre were for a while transferred to Harlem.

ELEVEN

TOWARDS THE CLOSE OF THE MINSTREL era and during the middle theatrical period the Negro in New York gained an important place among the makers of the nation's songs. For a century or more the Negro in America had been a folk-song maker. Black-face minstrelsy, in its beginnings, depended for its songs almost entirely on the Negro plantation jingles. In the earliest attempts to write songs for the minstrel stage there was merely slavish imitation or outright appropriation of this folk-material. It is plain that even so great a song-writer as Stephen Foster, who wrote his best songs when he lived in Cincinnati, just across the river from Kentucky, was greatly indebted to the enormous supply of Negro folk-song material at hand. But quite early the Negro emerged as an individual song-maker. Foster, America's first real song-writer, was at his height in the fifties; and in 1855 there appeared a song which became as popular and remains as lasting as any song he wrote, with the exception, perhaps, of "My Old Kentucky Home," "Old Folks at Home," and "Old Black Joe." In Philadelphia there lived a coloured barber named Richard Milburn, who worked in his father's shop on Lombard Street near Sixth. He was a guitar-player and a marvellous whistler, and it was he who originated the melody and at least the title of "Listen to the Mocking-Bird." Credit for this song is given to Septimus Winner (or to Alice Hawthorne, which was his mother's name, under which he published some of his compositions), but the truth is that Winner only set down the melody and arranged it after it had been played and whistled and sung over to him by Milburn. Winner or someone else may have furnished most or all of the words, but the life of the song springs from the melody. Old coloured residents of Philadelphia used to relate that before the song was ever published, Milburn played and whistled it at several gatherings, notably at a concert that was given at St. Thomas's Church, the coloured Episcopal church in Philadelphia. But the incontrovertible proof of Milburn's part in the making of the song is shown by its title-page as originally published by Winner and Shuster, under the copyright date of 1855, which reads: "Sentimental Ethiopian Ballad—*Listen To The Mocking Bird*—Melody by Richard Milburn—Written and arranged by Alice Hawthorne." The title-page of the song as published by Lee and Walker, under the copyright date of 1856, reads: "*Listen to the Mocking Bird*—As sung by Rose Merrifield—Written and arranged by Alice Hawthorne." Richard Milburn's name has not since appeared on the song.

One of the most popular of the minstrel songs of the seventies was "Carve dat 'Possum," written by Sam Lucas. Then from the ranks of the Negro minstrels there rose a really great song-writer in James Bland, who has already been mentioned. Bland wrote a long list of songs, of which four, at least, possess the qualities that entitle him to a place in the front rank of American song-writers. They are: "Carry Me Back to Old Virginny," "Oh, dem Golden Slippers," "In the Morning by the Brightlight," and "In the Evening by the Moonlight." Where is there the close-harmony quartet that has not revelled in the possibilities for barber-shop chords furnished by "In the Evening by the Moonlight" ? Frequently upon occasions "Carry Me Back to Old Virginny" is used in lieu of a state song. The bust of Patrick Henry was unveiled at the Hall of Fame May 8, 1930; die Governor of Virginia delivered the address of dedication, and immediately after the unveiling the trumpeters played "Carry Me Back to Old Virginny." All of Bland's songs hark back to the South—a South of tenderness and beauty. Following him came Gussie L. Davis, a typical New York writer, whose songs have not the slightest relation to the South or even to the Negro. Davis was a writer of popular ballads and as such had no superior, as anyone familiar with the songs of a generation ago will agree. Among many other songs he wrote: "Down in Poverty Row," "The Fatal Wedding," "In a Lighthouse by the Sea," "We Sat Beneath the Maple on the Hill," "Send Back the Picture and the Wedding Ring," and "The Baggage Coach Ahead."

The close of the nineties and the following decade was the high-watermark period of the coloured writers of popular songs in New York. Some were writers of only one or perhaps two songs that caught the public, and others wrote long lists of hits. Let those with an interest in the old songs muse for a moment over the following bit of cataloguing: Ernest Hogan wrote one song that swept this and other countries, a song which he, later in life, expressed regret at ever having written ; it was "All Coons Look Alike to Me." The melody of the song was beautiful and the words quite innocuous, but the title became a byword and an epithet of derision. Another writer of a single hit with a title that became a catch phrase was Al Johns, who wrote "Go 'Way Back and Sit Down." He wrote a number of other songs, some of them beautiful love ballads, but it was this musical oddity that brought him his moment of fame. Will Accoe wrote "My Samoan Beauty." Chris Smith, with R. C. McPherson doing the words, wrote "Good Morning, Carrie," a song with a melody that sang itself. Tim Brymn, with R. C. McPherson, wrote "Please Go 'Way and Let Me Sleep" and "Josephine, My Jo."

Sheppard Edmonds wrote "I'm Goin' to Live Anyhow until I Die." Irving Jones, a happy-go-lucky philosopher in song, wrote "I'm Living Easy" and "Take Your Clothes and Go." Williams and Walker had everybody singing "Dora Dean," "Why Don't You Get a Lady of Your Own," "I Don't Like No Cheap Man," "When It's All Goin' Out and Nothin' Comin' In," and other songs besides. The Cole and Johnson combination, through their collaboration on Broadway musical plays, wrote a string of popular hits. Among them were: "Under the Bamboo Tree," "The Congo Love Song," "The Maiden with the Dreamy Eyes," "Nobody's Looking but the Owl and the Moon," "Lazy Moon," "My Castle on the Nile," "I've Got Troubles of My Own," "Tell Me, Dusky Maiden," "I Must have been A-Dreaming," and "Oh, Didn't He Ramble?" The Cole and Johnson songs were sung by the most popular musical-comedy stars of the day: May Irwin, Marie Cahill, Fay Templeton, Lillian Russell, Anna Held, Virginia Earle, Marie George, Mabelle Gilman. Will Marion Cook wrote "Exhortation," "Rain Song," and "Bon Bon Buddy, the Chocolate Drop"—with words by Alex Rogers. Bert Williams, with Rogers, wrote "Jonah Man," "I May be Crazy but I Ain't No Fool," "Nobody," and "Why Adam Sinned"—better known, perhaps, as "Adam Never had no Mammy." There were also several writers of popular instrumental music, the outstanding one being Will Tyers, who wrote "La Trocha," "La Mariposa," and "Maori." This list of writers could be extended, as could the lists of songs by the several writers; but here is enough to indicate how important the Negro in New York came to be in the making of popular songs for the American people. There are at present a score or so of coloured writers of popular songs in New York actively at work in that profession. Outstanding among them are Jimmy Johnson, Spencer Williams, Andy Razaf and Thomas (Fats) Waller, who together wrote "My Fate is in Your Hands," which is now very popular, and Maceo Pinkard, who wrote "Mammy," a song made famous by Al Jolson. Eight or ten Negro writers are members of the American Society of Composers, Authors and Publishers, where they are received on an equal footing with others. This organization has for its purpose the collecting of royalty for the performance of music written by its members that may be performed in the theatres, broadcasting stations, hotels, restaurants, cabarets, and such places. There are similar societies in other countries, but the American society is the strongest in the world; last year it distributed among its members nearly a million and a half dollars.

In the mean time Harry T. Burleigh was writing songs which were to give him his place among American composers. In the work of writing the more musicianly songs J. Rosamond Johnson and Will Marion Cook also took part. These three men, unlike the other song-writers named, are thoroughly trained musicians. Mr. Burleigh was a student at the National Conservatory of Music in New York while Anton Dvorak was director. He studied harmony with Rubin Goldmark and counterpoint with Max Spicker. He not only studied with Dvorak, but spent a good deal of time with him at his home. It was he who called to the attention of the great Bohemian composer the *Negro Spirituals* and is therefore in that degree responsible for the part they play in the "New World" Symphony. In 1894 he had the unique distinction of being made baritone soloist at St. George's Church. Regarding this revolutionary innovation, Dr. William S. Rainsford, then rector of St. George's, says in his autobiography: "I broke the news to them [the St. George's choir] that I was going to have for soloist a Negro, Harry Burleigh. Then division, consternation, confusion, and protest reigned for a time. I never knew how the troubled waters settled down. Indeed, I carefully avoided knowing who was for and who against my revolutionary arrangement. Nothing like it had even been known in the church's musical history. The thing was arranged and I gave no opportunity for its discussion." The troubled waters did settle down, and Mr. Burleigh has held his position for now thirty-six years. In 1900 he became a member of the choir of Temple Emanu-El, at Fifth Avenue and Forty-third Street, and at the end of his twenty-fifth year was given an engrossed testimonial expressing the appreciation of the congregation for his services. He has written more than a hundred songs, besides his arrangements of the Spirituals. Among them are "Jean," "Little Mother of Mine," "Just You," "The Young Warrior," and "The Glory of the Day was in Her Face."

Mr. Johnson received his training at the New England Conservatory of Music, Boston. Mr. Cook studied at the Hochschule in Berlin, and the violin under Joachim. These two men have worked in both the popular and the more classical field, but their reputations have been gained chiefly in the former. Mr. Burleigh, on the other hand, has consistently stuck to the latter. Mr. Johnson has had a varied musical career and has shown great versatility. He has written the music for Negro musical comedies; he has written scores for white Broadway musical comedies; he was the Supervisor of Music at the London Opera House, Oscar Hammerstein's venture in the English metropolis; and when Messrs. Harris and Lasky attempted to give New York something more Parisian than anything in the French capital in *Hello Paris* at the Folies Bergere (now the Fulton Theatre), he wrote the music for that spicy revue, trained the members of the company, and conducted the orchestra, this being, it seems, the only time a Negro has conducted a white orchestra in a New York theatre for a play with a white cast. He has written songs of every description, from a Mississippi roustabout frolic like "Roll dem Cotton Bales" to a delicate love-song like "Three Questions." The best-known of his more ambitious songs are: "Sence You Went Away," "Lit'l Gal," and "The Awakening." He has arranged some hundred and fifty Negro Spirituals. But his most widely sung composition is "Lift Ev'ry Voice and Sing," a song that is used as a national hymn in coloured schools and churches and at Negro gatherings all over the country.

In the midst of the period we are now considering, another shift in the Negro population took place; and by 1900 there was a new centre established in West Fifty-third Street. In this new centre there sprang up a new phase of life among coloured New Yorkers. Two well-appointed hotels, the Marshall and the Maceo, run by coloured men, were opened in the street and became the centres of a fashionable sort of life that hitherto had not existed. These hotels served dinner to music and attracted crowds of well-dressed people. On Sunday evenings the crowd became a crush; and to be sure of service one had to book a table in advance. This new centre also brought about a revolutionary change in Negro artistic life. Those engaged in artistic effort deserted almost completely the old clubs farther downtown, and the Marshall, run by Jimmie Marshall, an accomplished Boniface, became famous as the headquarters of Negro talent. There gathered the actors, the musicians, the composers, the writers, and the better-paid vaudevillians; and there one went to get a close-up of Cole and Johnson, Williams and Walker, Ernest Hogan, Will Marion Cook, Jim Europe, Ada Overton, Abbie Mitchell, Al Johns, Theodore Drury, Will Dixon, and Ford Dabney. Paul Laurence Dunbar was often there. A good many white actors and musicians also frequented the Marshall, and it was no unusual thing for some among the biggest Broadway stars to run up there for an evening. So there were always present numbers of those who love to be in the light reflected from celebrities. Indeed, the Marshall for nearly ten years was one of the sights of New York, for it was gay, entertaining, and interesting. To be a visitor there, without at the same time being a rank outsider, was a distinction. The Maceo run by Benjamin F. Thomas had the more staid clientele.

In the brightest days of the Marshall the temporary blight had not yet fallen on the Negro in the theatre. Williams and Walker and Cole and Johnson were at their height; there were several good Negro road companies touring the country, and a considerable number of coloured performers were on the big time in vaudeville. In the early 1900's there came to the Marshall two young fellows, Ford Dabney and James Reese Europe, both of them from Washington, who were to play an important part in the artistic development of the Negro in a field that was, in a sense, new. It was they who first formed the coloured New York entertainers who played instruments into trained, organized bands, and thereby became not only the daddies of the Negro jazz orchestras, but the grand-daddies of the unnumbered jazz orchestras that have followed. Ford Dabney organized and directed a jazz orchestra which for a number of years was a feature of Florenz Ziegfeld's roof-garden shows. Jim Europe organized the Clef Club. Joe Jordan also became an important factor in the development of Negro bands.

How long Negro jazz bands throughout the country had been playing jazz at dances and in honky-tonks cannot be precisely stated, but the first modern jazz band ever heard on a New York stage, and probably on any other stage, was organized at the Marshall and made its debut at Proctor's Twenty-third Street Theatre in the early spring of 1905. It was a playing-singing-dancing orchestra, making dominant use of banjos, mandolins, guitars, saxophones, and drums in combination, and was called the Memphis Students—a very good name, overlooking the fact that the performers were not students and were not from Memphis. There was also a violin, a couple of brass instruments, and a double-bass.

The band was made up of about twenty of the best performers on the instruments mentioned above that could be got together in New York. They had all been musicians and entertainers for private parties, and as such had played together in groups varying in size, according to the amount the employing host wished to spend. Will Marion Cook gave a hand in whipping them into shape for their opening. They scored an immediate success. After the Proctor engagement they went to Hammerstein's *Victoria*, playing on the vaudeville bill in the day, and on the roof-garden at night. In the latter part of the same year they opened at Olympia in Paris; from Paris they went to the Palace Theatre in London, and then to the Schumann Circus in Berlin. They played all the important cities of Europe and were abroad a year.

At the opening in New York the performers who were being counted on to carry the stellar honours were: Ernest Hogan, comedian; Abbie Mitchell, soprano; and Ida Forsyne, dancer; but while they made good, the band proved to be the thing. The instrumentalists were the novelty. There was one thing they did quite unconsciously; which, however, caused musicians who heard them to marvel at the feat. When the band played and sang, there were men who played one part while singing another. That is, for example, some of them while playing the lead, sang bass, and some while playing an alto part sang tenor; and so on, in accordance with the instrument each man played and his natural voice. The Memphis Students deserve the credit that should go to pioneers. They were the beginners of several things that still persist as jazz- band features. They introduced the dancing conductor. Will Dixon, himself a composer of some note, conducted the band here and on its European tour. All through a number he would keep his men together by dancing out the rhythm, generally in graceful, sometimes in grotesque, steps. Often an easy shuffle would take him across the whole front of the band. This style of directing not only got the fullest possible response from the men, but kept them in just the right humour for the sort of music they were playing. Another innovation they introduced was the trick trap-drummer. "Buddy" Gilmore was the drummer with the band, and it is doubtful if he has been surpassed as a performer of juggling and acrobatic stunts while manipulating a dozen noise-making devices aside from the drums. He made this style of drumming so popular that not only was it adopted by white professionals, but many white amateurs undertook to learn it as a social accomplishment, just as they might learn to do card tricks. The whole band, with the exception, of course, of the players on wind-instruments, was a singing band; and it seems safe to say that they introduced the singing band—that is, a band singing in four-part harmony and playing at the same time.

One of the original members of the Memphis Students was Jim Europe. Afterwards he went for a season or two as the musical director with the Cole and Johnson shows; and then in the same capacity with Bert Williams's *Mr. Lode of Kole*. In 1910 he carried out an idea he had, an idea that had a business as well as an artistic reason behind it, and organized the Clef Club. He gathered all the coloured professional instrumental musicians into a chartered organization and systematized the whole business of "entertaining." The organization purchased a house in West Fifty-third Street and fitted it up as a club, and also as booking-offices. Bands of from three to thirty men could be furnished at any time, day or night. The Clef Club for quite a while held a monopoly of the business of "entertaining" private parties and furnishing music for the dance craze, which was then just beginning to sweep the country. One year the amount of business done amounted to $120,000.

The crowning artistic achievement of the Clef Club was a concert given at Carnegie Hall in May 1912. The orchestra for the occasion consisted of one hundred and twenty-five performers. It was an unorthodox combination—as is every true jazz orchestra. There were a few strings proper, the most of them being 'cellos and double-basses; the few wind-instruments consisted of cornets, saxophones, clarinets, and trombones; there was a battery of drums; but the main part of the orchestra was composed of banjos, mandolins, and guitars. On this night all these instruments were massed against a background of ten upright pianos. In certain parts the instrumentation was augmented by the voices. New York had not yet become accustomed to jazz; so when the Clef Club opened its concert with a syncopated march, playing it with a biting attack and an infectious rhythm, and on the finale bursting into singing, the effect can be imagined. The applause became a tumult. It is possible that such a band as that could produce a similar effect even today.

Later Jim Europe with his orchestra helped to make Vernon and Irene Castle famous. When the World War came, he assembled the men for the band of the Fifteenth, New York's noted Negro regiment. He was with this band giving a concert in a Boston theatre, after their return from the War, when he met his tragic end.

1912 was also the year in which there came up out of the South an entirely new genre of Negro songs, one that was to make an immediate and lasting effect upon American popular music; namely, the blues. These songs are as truly folk-songs as the Spirituals, or as the original plantation songs, levee songs, and rag-time songs that had already been made the foundation of our national popular music. The blues were first set down and published by William C. Handy, a coloured composer and for a while a bandleader in Memphis, Tennessee. He put out the famous "Memphis Blues" and the still more famous "St. Louis Blues" and followed them by blues of many localities and kinds. It was not long before the New York song-writers were turning out blues of every variety and every shade. Handy followed the blues to New York and has been a Harlemite ever since, where he is known as the "Father of the Blues." It is from the blues that all that may be called *American music* derives its most distinctive characteristic.

It was during the period we have just been discussing that the earliest attempt at rendering opera was made by Negroes in New York. Beginning in the first half of the decade 1900–10 and continuing for four or five years, the Theodore Drury Opera Company gave annually one night of grand opera at the Lexington Opera House. Among the operas sung were *Carmen, Aida,* and *Faust.* These nights of grand opera were, at least, great social affairs and were looked forward to months ahead. In September 1928 H. Lawrence Freeman, a Negro musician and the composer of six grand operas, produced his opera *Voodoo* at the Fifty-second Street Theatre. Mr. Freeman's operas are *The Martyr, The Prophecy, The Octoroon, Plantation, Vendetta,* and *Voodoo.* In the spring of the present year he presented scenes from various of his works in Steinway Hall. He was the winner of the 1929 Harmon Award and Medal for musical composition.

TWELVE

THE YEAR 1900 MARKED ANOTHER EPOCH for the Negro in New York. On the night of August 12, a coloured man named Arthur Harris left his wife on the corner of Eighth Avenue and Forty-first Street for a moment to buy a cigar. When he returned he found her struggling in the grasp of a white man. Harris engaged with the man and was struck by him over the head with a club. He retaliated with a pocket-knife and inflicted a wound which proved fatal. He thereupon ran away. The white man was Robert J. Thorpe, a police officer in plain clothes, who claimed that he had arrested the woman for "soliciting." Thorpe was very popular with his brother officers, and his funeral was attended by a large contingent of the police force, in addition to a great throng of friends, sympathizers, and those drawn by morbid curiosity. Harris had disappeared; and during the day of the funeral the temper of the crowd to wreak vengeance upon some vicarious victim grew strong. As the day closed, rumours that there was going to be trouble flew faster and faster.

Early in the evening of August 15 the fourth great New York race riot burst in full fury. A mob of several thousands raged up and down Eighth Avenue and through the side streets from Twenty-seventh to Forty-second. Negroes were seized wherever they were found, and brutally beaten. Men and women were dragged from street-cars and assaulted. When Negroes ran to policemen for protection, even begging to be locked up for safety, they were thrown back to the mob. The police themselves beat many Negroes as cruelly as did the mob. An intimate friend of mine was one of those who ran to the police for protection; he received such a clubbing at their hands that he had to be taken to the hospital to have his scalp stitched in several places. It was a beating from which he never fully recovered.

During the height of the riot the cry went out to "get Ernest Hogan and Williams and Walker and Cole and Johnson." These seemed to be the only individual names the crowd was familiar with. Ernest Hogan was at the time playing at the New York Winter Garden, in Times Square; for safety he was kept in the theatre all night. George Walker had a narrow escape. The riot of 1900 was a brutish orgy, which, if it was not incited by the police, was, to say the least, abetted by them.

But this fourth of the great New York riots involving the Negro was really symptomatic of a national condition. The status of the Negro as a citizen had been steadily declining for twenty-five years; and at the opening of the twentieth century his civil state was, in some respects, worse than at the close of the Civil War. At the opening of the twentieth century the War Amendments passed in the Negro's behalf had been completely nullified or evaded in the Southern states; and he was disfranchised, "Jim Crowed," outraged, and denied the equal protection of the laws. In the decade ending in 1899, according to the records printed in the daily press, 1,665 Negroes were lynched, many of them with sadistic savagery, even by mutilation and by burning alive at the stake in the presence of great crowds. And these debauches in bestiality aroused no action on the part of the country nor any general protest. The outlook was dark and discouraging. The Negro himself had in a large measure lost heart. The movement that Frederick Douglass had so valiantly carried forward had all but subsided. The general spirit of the race was one of hopelessness or acquiescence. The only way to survival seemed along the road of sheer opportunism and of conformity to the triumphant materialism of the age. Idealism linked with courage was scarcely discernible. Nor did these conditions pertain solely to the South. The South lost the Civil War in 1865, but by 1900, in the fight waged on the Negro battle front, it had conquered the North; and all through the old free states there was a tendency to concede that the grand experiment was a failure.

Nowhere in the country was this decline in the spirit of self-assertion of rights more marked than in New York. A comparison between the times of Douglass, Garnett, and Crummell and the opening of the new century was like a comparison between the light of a tropic noon and a winter twilight. But the riot of 1900 woke Negro New York and stirred the old fighting spirit.

The answer to demands for an investigation of the riot was a series of excuses and delays on the part of the municipality and the police authorities; then the coloured citizens took steps to force action. A meeting was called at St. Mark's Church in West Fifty-third Street, and the Citizens Protective League was organized. The Rev. William H. Brooks, the pastor of the church, was made president; James E. Garner, a successful business man, was made treasurer; and T. Thomas Fortune was elected chairman of the executive committee. Mr. Fortune was editor of the New York *Age*, the oldest Negro newspaper in New York, and a writer of marked ability. For many years he was the acknowledged leader in the Negro newspaper world; and for a while he contributed a regular column to the New York *Sun*. In ability and courage he was a direct descendant of the leaders of twenty-five years before. The Citizens Protective League held a mass meeting in Carnegie Hall on

September 12, and funds were raised. The organization retained a lawyer to prosecute police officers; and its membership grew to about five thousand. The league in a letter to Mayor Van Wyck demanded the conviction and removal from the force of those officers it was able to prove guilty of malfeasance or nonfeasance. The Mayor replied that the whole matter was in the hands of the Police Board. Finally an investigation was held in which coloured citizens who testified to having been beaten by the police were themselves treated as persons accused of crime, and the testimony of each was simply rebutted by policemen who were called to testify. The investigation turned out to be a sham and a whitewash; nevertheless, the Negroes of New York, moved by this sudden realization of their danger, had taken a step towards making that city anew the chief radiating centre of the forces contending for equal rights.

A promising move in this same direction had been made in 1889, when T. Thomas Fortune issued a call for the formation of the thinking and progressive coloured people of the country into a national organization to protest against the increasing disabilities and injustices to which the race was being subjected. The call was answered by one hundred and forty-one delegates from twenty-one states, who met in Chicago, January 15, 1890, and organized the Afro-American Council. J. C. Price, the head of Livingstone College in North Carolina, a man who had achieved considerable prestige as a leader, was chosen president, and T. Thomas Fortune, secretary. The following year the council met at Knoxville, Tennessee, and Mr. Fortune succeeded Mr. Price as president. The organization then lay dormant until 1898, when Bishop Alexander Walters, of New York, stirred by fresh outrages against Negroes, issued a call to Mr. Fortune to reassemble the council. The result was a meeting on September 15 of the same year at Rochester,

New York, with one hundred and fifty delegates present, at the time when the monument to Frederick Douglass was being unveiled in that city. Another meeting was held at Washington in December to finish the business of the Rochester meeting. But the Afro-American Council did not realize its aim; it found it impossible to arouse the sort of spirit and response on the part of the coloured people of the country necessary for the real growth of the organization; nor was it able to raise sufficient funds to create a permanent and efficient machine; so after a somewhat languishing existence of several years longer, it died. But it had accomplished something; it had pointed the way—not a new one but the old one—and it was to be followed by a similar effort made in what was more nearly the fullness of time.

In 1895 Booker T. Washington made his epochal Atlanta speech. He had for ten years prior to that occasion been a rising figure, but after it his increase in power and prestige was so rapid that almost immediately he found himself the recognized leader of the Negro race. By his Atlanta speech he had at a stroke gained the sanction and support of both the South and the North—the South, in general, construing the speech to imply the Negro's abdication of his claim to full and equal citizenship rights, and his acceptance of the status of a contented and industrious peasantry; the North feeling that the opportunity had arisen to rid its conscience of a disturbing question and shift it over to the South. The great body of the Negroes, discouraged, bewildered, and leaderless, hailed Mr. Washington as a Moses. This was, indeed, a remarkable feat—his holding the South in one hand, the North in the other, and at the same time carrying the major portion of his race along with him. The feat of uniting these three factions in the attempt to benefit the third had been tried before, but never achieved; and the founder of Tuskegee was the first to approach an accomplishment of it.

The fact that he succeeded so far as he did, notwithstanding the popular conception of him as only an earnest educator and an energetic builder, stamps him as one of the world's ablest diplomats. At the height of his career Booker T. Washington was by long odds the most distinguished man the South had produced after the era following that of the Civil War heroes. There can hardly be an intelligent American who would not be thrilled by the sheer romance of his life's story. Born a slave amidst a squalor and poverty difficult to describe; as a child sleeping "in and on a bundle of filthy rags laid upon the dirt floor";[1] knowing nothing of his father, and set free at emancipation a ragged, illiterate, penniless bit of humanity, not possessing even a name beyond Booker; he rose to make the name of his own taking known throughout the world and to acquire a degree of power and influence second to that of no private individual in the country. Born in a log cabin where there was no such thing as a table, but where the children were handed a piece of bread here and a scrap of meat there, he lived to sit at table with the President of the United States, and to sip tea with the Queen of England. There is no more magical page in the *Arabian Nights*.

Dr. Washington encountered criticism from men of his own race. His critics felt that he was yielding more than what would be the ultimate worth of what he gained. The criticism grew louder, but it was not formulated, and the dissenters were without an authoritative voice. There was criticism of the fact that the doctrine of industrial education had been interpreted as meaning that it was the only education the Negro race would need to fit it for the place it was to occupy. There was also criticism of the minifying of political and civil rights. Over against these criticisms stood the great, concrete demonstration, Tuskegee;

1. Booker T. Washington: *Up from Slavery*. New York, Doubleday, Page and Company.

endorsed by the South, supported by the North, and not only doing a tremendous work for the Negroes of the South, but wielding an increasing influence on educational ideas with regard to the white youth of the country. In the face of these solid achievements the criticisms took on a doctrinaire aspect, an aspect of bickering and faultfinding.

In 1903 a book came out of Atlanta, written by a professor at Atlanta University. The book was *The Souls of Black Folk*, and the author was W. E. Burghardt Du Bois. The author of *The Souls of Black Folk*, like the author of *Up from Slavery*, was a Negro, but, aside from that, their antecedents were quite different. Du Bois was born two years after the close of the Civil War in a beautiful, cultured New England town, Great Barrington, Massachusetts. He was educated in the grammar and high schools of his native town; then at Fisk University; then at Harvard; and then at the University of Berlin. He experienced the pride of knowing his ancestry; three generations of his forebears lay in the Great Barrington cemetery. When he began active life, it was with greater intellectual preparation than any American Negro had yet acquired. This book of his was at once hailed as a great book. It was a collection of essays, one of which was headed "Of Mr. Washington and Others " and contained an estimate of Booker T. Washington and a statement of the points on which the author differed with him. Because of the criticism it voiced, this chapter in the book immediately became the subject of a nation-wide controversy, especially sharp in the South; and the guns of criticism were turned upon Du Bois. But the chief significance of this essay lies in the effect wrought by it within the race. It brought about a coalescence of the more radical elements and made them articulate, thereby creating a split of the race into two contending camps, between which there has been a *rapprochement* only within the past ten years—a *rapprochement* achieved mostly through the moving over of the conservative group. And so, with the issuance of a book from Atlanta, a new leader stepped forth; and Du Bois found himself at the head of the scattered and almost silent remnants of the old militant Negro element.

Dr. Du Bois planned to bring the Negro militants together, and in answer to a call sent out by him, a conference was held, July 11–13, 1905, at Buffalo, New York. Twenty-nine coloured men were present from thirteen states and the District of Columbia. Three states of the old South—Georgia, Tennessee, and Virginia—were represented. A national organization was formed and called "the Niagara Movement." In the constitution that was adopted the following objects were stated: (a) freedom of speech and criticism; (b) an unfettered and unsubsidized press; (c) manhood suffrage; (d) the abolition of all caste distinctions based simply on race and colour; (e) the recognition of the principles of human brotherhood as a practical present creed; (f) the recognition of the highest and best human training as the monopoly of no class or race; (g) a belief in the dignity of labour; (h) united effort to realize these ideals under wise and courageous leadership.

The following year, in August, the Niagara Movement met at Harpers Ferry, the scene of John Brown's martyrdom, and adopted and sent out *An Address to the Country*, which, in part, read:

> The men of the Niagara Movement coming from the toil of the year's hard work and pausing for a moment from the earning of their daily bread turn toward the nation and again ask in the name of ten million the privilege of a hearing. In the past year the work of the Negro hater has flourished in the land. Step by step the defenders of the rights of American citizens have retreated. The work of stealing the black man's

ballot has progressed and the fifty and more representatives of stolen votes still sit in the nation's capital. Discrimination in travel and public accommodation has so spread that some of our weaker brethren are actually afraid to thunder against color discrimination as such and are simply whispering for ordinary decencies.

Against this the Niagara Movement eternally protests. We will not be satisfied to take one jot or tittle less than our full manhood rights. We claim for ourselves every single right that belongs to a freeborn American, political, civil and social; and until we get these rights we will never cease to protest and assail the ears of America. The battle we wage is not for ourselves alone but for all true Americans. It is a fight for ideals, lest this, our common fatherland, false to its founding, become in truth the land of the thief and the home of the Slave—a by-word and a hissing among the nations for its sounding pretensions and pitiful accomplishment.

Never before in the modem age has a great and civilized folk threatened to adopt so cowardly a creed in the treatment of its fellow-citizens born and bred on its soil. Stripped of verbiage and subterfuge and in its naked nastiness the new American creed says: Fear to let black men even try to rise lest they become the equals of the white. And this is the land that professes to follow Jesus Christ. The blasphemy of such a course is only matched by its cowardice.

In detail our demands are clear and unequivocal. First, we would vote; with the right to vote goes everything: Freedom, manhood, the honor of your wives, the chastity of your daughters, the right to work, and the chance to rise, and let no man listen to those who deny this.

We want full manhood suffrage, and we went it now, henceforth and forever.

Second. We want discrimination in public accommodation to cease. Separation in railway and street cars, based simply on race and color, is un-American, undemocratic, and silly. We protest against all such discrimination.

Third. We claim the right of freemen to walk, talk, and be with them that wish to be with us. No man has a right to choose another man's friends, and to attempt to do so is an impudent interference with the most fundamental human privilege.

Fourth. We want the laws enforced against rich as well as poor; against Capitalist as well as Laborer; against white as well as black. We are not more lawless than the white race, we are more often arrested, convicted, and mobbed. We want justice even for criminals and outlaws. We want the Constitution of the country enforced. We want Congress to take charge of Congressional elections. We want the Fourteenth amendment carried out to the letter and every State disfranchised in Congress which attempts to disfranchise its rightful voters. We want the Fifteenth amendment enforced and no State allowed to base its franchise simply on color.

The failure of the Republican Party in Congress at the session just closed to redeem its pledge of 1904 with reference to suffrage conditions at the South seems a plain, deliberate, and premeditated breach of promise, and stamps that party as guilty of obtaining votes under false pretenses.

Fifth. We want our children educated. The school system

in the country districts of the South is a disgrace and in few towns and cities are the Negro schools what they ought to be. We want the national government to step in and wipe out illiteracy in the South. Either the United States will destroy ignorance or ignorance will destroy the United States.

And when we call for education we mean real education. We believe in work. We ourselves are workers, but work is not necessarily education. Education is the development of power and ideal. We want our children trained as intelligent human beings should be, and we will fight for all time against any proposal to educate black boys and girls simply as servants and underlings, or simply for the use of other people. They have a right to know, to think, to aspire.

These are some of the chief things which we want. How shall we get them? By voting where we may vote, by persistent, unceasing agitation; by hammering at the truth, by sacrifice and work.

Reading today the chapter from *The Souls of Black Folk*, "Of Mr. Washington and Others," it is, perhaps, impossible for those unfamiliar with the period to understand the extent of the reaction it caused and the bitterness of the animosities it aroused. The latter, at any rate, was due to causes not specifically contained in what Dr. Du Bois had written, but outside of it. The essay was not an attack. It contained no word of denunciation. Neither was there in it invective or irony, two of the author's favourite and most effective weapons. It was, in fact, a temperate analysis of Dr. Washington's position and policy and a rationally stated difference on certain points. The spirit of the whole essay can be fairly illustrated by two quotations, one near the beginning and the other near the end:

> To gain the sympathy and cooperation of the various elements comprising the white South was Mr. Washington's first task; and this, at the time Tuskegee was founded, seemed, for a black man impossible. And yet ten years later it was done in the word spoken at Atlanta: "In all things purely social we can be as separate as the five fingers, and yet one as the hand in all things essential to material progress." This "Atlanta Compromise " is by all odds the most notable thing in Mr. Washington's career. The South interpreted it in different ways: the radicals received it as a complete surrender of the demand for civil and political equality; the conservatives as a generously conceived working basis for mutual understanding. So both approved it, and today its author is certainly the most distinguished Southerner since Jefferson Davis, and the one with the greatest personal following. . . .
>
> The black men of America have a duty to perform, a duty stem and delicate,—a forward movement to oppose a part of the work of their greatest leader. So far as Mr. Washington preaches Thrift, Patience and Industrial Training for the masses, we must hold up his hands and strive with him, rejoicing in his honours and glorying in the strength of this Joshua called of God and of man to lead the headless host. But so far as Mr. Washington apologizes for injustice, North or South, does not rightly value the privilege and duty of voting, belittles the emasculating effects of caste distinctions, and opposes the higher training

and ambition of our brightest minds,—so far as he, the South, or the nation, does this,—we must increasingly and firmly oppose them.

Much has happened and many changes have occurred in the North and in the South since those words were written. Last year the present head of Tuskegee, Dr. R. R. Moton, wrote a book, *What the Negro Thinks*,[2] which was in substance a restatement of the objects set forth by the Niagara Movement; and in answer he received words of approbation from the Southern press. The two groups once so sharply divided are today practically one, with regard to the fundamental aims of the American Negro. Dr. Moton says in his book: "In truth, they are working for the same thing in different spheres and by a different approach." In truth they have learned that a co-ordinated plan of battle calls for the militants to act as shock troops and for the conservatives to advance rapidly and hold the ground.

One of the visitors at the Harpers Ferry meeting of the Niagara Movement was Miss Mary White Ovington of New York, one of the few remaining inheritors of the abolition spirit, who had for several years been studying the condition of the Negro in the North and in the South. She went to report the conference for the New York *Evening Post*. In the fall of 1908, William English Walling had an article in the *Independent* on the race riots which had recently taken place in Springfield, Illinois, Abraham Lincoln's old home, in which Negroes had been beaten and killed in the streets of that city. After describing the brutalities committed upon coloured people in that outbreak, Mr. Walling declared: "Either the spirit

2. Robert Russa Moton: *What the Negro Thinks*. Garden City, Doubleday, Doran and Company, 1929.

of the abolitionists, of Lincoln and of Lovejoy, must be revived and we must come to treat the Negro on a plane of absolute political and social equality or Vardaman and Tillman will soon have transferred the Race War to the North." Miss Ovington wrote to Mr. Walling and later talked with him over the matter, together with Dr. Henry Moskowitz, early in January 1909. Plans were discussed for making a demonstration on February 12, the one hundredth anniversary of Abraham Lincoln's birth. Oswald Garrison Villard joined with the movement, and on Lincoln's birthday a call for a conference, drafted by Mr. Villard, was issued. Among the liberal whites who signed the call were Charles Edward Russell, Jane Addams, Samuel Bowles, John Dewey, Mary E. McDowell, John Haynes Holmes, Florence Kelley, Lillian D. Wald, John E. Milholland, Rabbi Stephen S. Wise, and William Dean Howells. Among the Negro liberals who joined in were Dr. W. E. Burghardt Du Bois, Bishop Alexander Walters, Ida Wells Barnett, and the Rev. Francis J. Grimke.

Charles Edward Russell, who had also talked with Mr. Walling following the appearance of the *Independent* article, was the presiding genius at the more or less stormy closing sessions of this first conference, when a temporary organization was formed. In May 1910 a second conference was held, in New York, at which there was consummated a merger of the forces of the Negro liberals of the Niagara Movement, and the white liberals of abolition traditions, thus forming the National Association for the Advancement of Colored People. The platform adopted was practically the same as that of the Niagara Movement. It was commented upon at the time as being extremely radical. In this same year the association called Dr. Du Bois to come as its Director of Publicity and Research. He resigned his professorship at Atlanta University and came to New York; and the publication of the *Crisis*, a monthly magazine, the organ of the association, with Dr. Du Bois as editor, was begun. The *Crisis* has now been doing pioneer work for twenty years; and Dr. Du Bois, more than any other one man, paved the way for the "New Negro." At about this time two other strong friends became allied with the movement, J. E. Spingarn and Arthur B. Spingarn.

The association has grown to be a powerful and effective organization. It has national headquarters in New York City and more than three hundred branches in forty-four states. Its record of accomplishment in the past twenty years is extraordinary. Besides its work in legal defence and its fight against lynching and against discriminations in the administration of the law, in facilities for education, and in the use of common carriers and places of public accommodation, it has carried to the United States Supreme Court and won four important and far-reaching decisions affecting the constitutional and citizenship rights of the American Negro. These were decisions in: the Louisville segregation case, the Arkansas peonage cases, the Texas white primary case, and the New Orleans segregation case. In addition it had a hand in winning the "grandfather clause " case.[3] One of the reasons for this degree of success in prosecuting the Negro's cause through the courts has been the fact that the association had the voluntary services of such lawyers as Moorfield Storey, Louis Marshall, Clarence Darrow, James A. Cobb, Charles H. Studin, and Arthur B. Spingarn as members of its legal committee.

The National Association for the Advancement of Colored People was the first and is still the only organization since the Anti-Slavery

3. "Grandfather clauses" began to be adopted in the constitutions of Southern states in 1898. They were disfranchising devices, in that they laid down as necessary to the right of suffrage a list of property, literacy, and character qualifications; and then provided that none of these qualifications need be met by any person who had the right to vote or had an ancestor who had the right to vote at the time of the close of the Civil War. The Supreme Court declared these clauses unconstitutional in 1915.

Society providing a common medium for the co-operation of blacks and whites in the work of securing and safeguarding the common citizenship rights of the Negro. With the founding of this association New York became again the centre of the organized forces of self-assertion of equal rights and of insistence upon the impartial application of the fundamental principles of the Republic, without regard to race, creed, or colour.

Shortly following the formation of the Advancement Association steps were taken which led to the establishment of another important national organization to work for the Negro, with headquarters in New York, the National League on Urban Conditions among Negroes. Among those who took part in the founding of the organization were: Mrs. Ruth Standish Baldwin, Edwin R. A. Seligman, Fred R. Moore, Miss Elizabeth Walton, L. Hollingsworth Wood, George E. Haynes, and Eugene Kinckle Jones. The main purpose for which this organization was formed was to work for the industrial, social, and health betterment of the coloured people, especially those living in urban centres. In addition to working for these ends, the Urban League has carried on research work and collected a great deal of valuable data and statistics on industrial, social, and health conditions among Negroes. It has grown rapidly and now has affiliated branches in the principal cities in all sections of the country. Each of these branch offices is manned by a trained secretary and social workers. The Urban League, like the Advancement Association, is an organization in which both races co-operate.

Ten years after the forming of these two bodies another organization destined to make Negro history in New York was in full swing—the Garvey movement.

The Negro population in 1910 of all the boroughs of the city was 91,709; and of Manhattan alone, 60,534.

THIRTEEN

I F YOU RIDE NORTHWARD THE LENGTH of Manhattan Island, going through Central Park and coming out on Seventh Avenue or Lenox Avenue at One Hundred and Tenth Street, you cannot escape being struck by the sudden change in the character of the people you see. In the middle and lower parts of the city you have, perhaps, noted Negro faces here and there; but when you emerge from the Park, you see them everywhere, and as you go up either of these two great arteries leading out from the city to the north, you see more and more Negroes, walking in the streets, looking from the windows, trading in the shops, eating in the restaurants, going in and coming out of the theatres, until, nearing One Hundred and Thirty-fifth Street, ninety per cent of the people you see, including the traffic officers, are Negroes. And it is not until you cross the Harlem River that the population whitens again, which it does as suddenly as it began to darken at One Hundred and Tenth Street. You have been having an outside glimpse of Harlem, the Negro metropolis.

In nearly every city in the country the Negro section is a nest or several nests situated somewhere on the borders; it is a section one must "go out to." In New York it is entirely different. Negro Harlem is situated in the heart of Manhattan and covers one of the most beautiful and healthful sites in the whole city. It is not a fringe, it is not a slum, nor is it a "quarter" consisting of dilapidated tenements. It is a section of new-law apartment houses and handsome dwellings, with streets as well paved, as well lighted, and as well kept as in any other part of the city. Three main highways lead into and out from upper Manhattan, and two of them run straight through Harlem. So Harlem is not a section that one "goes out to," but a section that one goes through.

Roughly drawn, the boundaries of Harlem are: One Hundred and Tenth Street on the south; on the east, Lenox Avenue to One Hundred and Twenty-sixth Street, then Lexington Avenue to the Harlem River, and the Harlem River on the east and north to a point where it passes the Polo Grounds, just above One Hundred and Fifty-fifth Street; on the west, Eighth Avenue to One Hundred and Sixteenth Street, then St. Nicholas Avenue up to a juncture with the Harlem River at the Polo Grounds. To the east of the Lenox Avenue boundary there are a score of blocks of mixed coloured and white population; and to the west of the Eighth Avenue boundary there is a solid Negro border, two blocks wide, from One Hundred and Sixteenth Street to One Hundred and Twenty-fifth Street. The heights north from One Hundred and Forty-fifth Street, known as Coogan's Bluff, are solidly black. Within this area of less than two square miles live more than two hundred thousand Negroes, more to the square acre than in any other place on earth.

This city within a city, in these larger proportions, is actually a development of the last fifteen years. The trek to Harlem began when the West Fifty- third Street centre had reached its utmost development; that is, early in the decade 1900–10. The move to West Fifty-third Street had been the result of the opportunity to get into better houses; and the move to Harlem was due to the same urge. In fact, Harlem offered the coloured people the first chance in their entire history in New

York to live in modem apartment houses. West Fifty-third Street was superior to anything they had ever enjoyed; and there they were, for the most part, making private dwellings serve the purpose of apartments, housing several families in each house. The move to Harlem, in the beginning and for a long time, was fathered and engineered by Philip A. Payton, a coloured man in the real-estate business. But this was more than a matter of mere business with Mr. Payton; the matter of better and still better housing for coloured people in New York became the dominating idea of his life, and he worked on it as long as he lived. When Negro New Yorkers evaluate their benefactors in their own race, they must find that not many have done more than Phil Payton; for much of what has made Harlem the intellectual and artistic capital of the Negro world is in good part due to this fundamental advantage: Harlem has provided New York Negroes with better, cleaner, more modern, more airy, more sunny houses than they ever lived in before. And this is due to the efforts made first by Mr. Payton.

Harlem had been overbuilt with new apartment houses. It was far uptown, and the only rapid transportation was the elevated running up Eighth Avenue—the Lenox Avenue Subway had not yet been built. This left the people on Lenox Avenue and to the east with only the electric street-cars convenient. So landlords were finding it hard to fill their houses on that side of the section. Mr. Payton approached several of these landlords with the proposal to fill their empty houses with coloured tenants and keep them filled. Economic necessity usually discounts race prejudice—or any other kind of prejudice—as much as ninety per cent, sometimes a hundred; so the landlords with empty houses whom Mr. Payton approached accepted his proposal, and one or two houses on One Hundred and Thirty-fourth Street were taken over and filled with coloured tenants. Gradually other houses were filled. The white residents of the section showed very little concern about the movement until it began to spread to the west and across Lenox Avenue; then they took steps to check it. They organized, and formed plans to purchase through the Hudson Realty Company, a financial concern, all properties occupied by coloured people and evict the tenants. Payton countered by forming the Afro-American Realty Company, a Negro corporation organized for the purpose of buying and leasing houses to be let to coloured tenants. This counterstroke held the opposition in check for several years and enabled the Negroes to hold their own.

But the steady and increasing pressure of Negroes across the Lenox Avenue deadline caused the opposition to break out anew; and this time the plans were more deeply laid and more difficult for the Negroes to defeat. These plans, formulated by several leading spirits, involved what was actually a conspiracy—the organization of whites to bring pressure on financial institutions to lend no money and renew no mortgages on properties occupied by coloured people. These plans had considerable success and reached beyond the situation they were formed to deal with. They still furnish one of the hardest and most unjustifiable handicaps the Negro property- owner in Harlem has to contend with.

The Afro-American Realty Company, for lack of the large amount of capital essential, was now defunct; but several individual coloured men carried on. Philip A. Payton and J. C. Thomas bought two five-story apartments, dispossessed the white tenants, and put in coloured ones. John B. Nail bought a row of five apartments and did the same. St. Philip's Episcopal Church, one of the oldest and richest coloured congregations in New York, bought a row of thirteen apartments on One Hundred and Thirty-fifth Street between Lenox and Seventh

Avenues and rented them to coloured tenants. The situation now resolved itself into an actual contest. But the Negro pressure continued constant. Coloured people not only continued to move into apartments outside the zone east of Lenox Avenue, but began to purchase the fine private houses between Lenox and Seventh. Then, in the eyes of the whites who were antagonistic, the whole movement took on the aspect of an "invasion"—an invasion of both their economic and their social rights. They felt that Negroes as neighbours not only lowered the values of their property, but also lowered their social status. Seeing that they could not stop the movement, they began to flee. They took fright, they became panic-stricken, they ran amuck. Their conduct could be compared to that of a community in the Middle Ages fleeing before an epidemic of the black plague, except for the fact that here the reasons were not so sound. But these people did not stop to reason, they did not stop to ask why they did what they were doing, or what would happen if they didn't do it. The presence of a single coloured family in a block, regardless of the fact that they might be well-bred people, with sufficient means to buy their new home, was a signal for precipitate flight. The stampeded whites actually deserted house after house and block after block. Then prices dropped; they dropped lower than the bottom, and such coloured people as were able took advantage of these prices and bought. Some of the banks and lending companies that were compelled to take over deserted houses for the mortgages they held refused for a time to either sell or rent them to Negroes. Instead, they proposed themselves to bear the carrying charges and hold them vacant for what they evidently hoped would be a temporary period. Prices continued to drop. And this was the property situation in Harlem at the outbreak of the World War in Europe.

With the outbreak of the war there came a sudden change. One of the first effects of the war was to draw thousands of aliens out of this country back to their native lands to join the colours. Naturally, there was also an almost total cessation of immigration. Moreover, the United States was almost immediately called upon to furnish munitions and supplies of all kinds to the warring countries. The result of these converging causes was an unprecedented shortage of labour and a demand that was imperative. From whence could the necessary supply be drawn? There was only one source, and that was the reservoir of black labour in the South. And it was at once drawn on to fill the existing vacuum in the great industries of the North. Every available method was used to get these black hands, the most effective being the sending of labour agents into the South, who dealt directly with the Negroes, arranged for their transportation, and shipped them north, often in single consignments running high up into the hundreds. I witnessed the sending north from a Southern city in one day a crowd estimated at twenty-five hundred. They were shipped on a train run in three sections, packed in day coaches, with all their baggage and other impedimenta. The exodus was on, and migrants came north in thousands, tens of thousands, hundreds of thousands—from the docks of Norfolk, Savannah, Jacksonville, Tampa, Mobile, New Orleans, and Galveston; from the cotton fields of Mississippi, and the coal-mines and steel mills of Alabama and Tennessee; from workshops and washtubs and brick-yards and kitchens they came, until the number, by conservative estimate, went well over the million and a half mark. For the Negroes of the South this was the happy blending of desire with opportunity.

It could not be otherwise in such a wholesale migration than that many who came were ignorant, inefficient, and worthless, and that there was also a proportion of downright criminals. But industry was in no position to be fastidious; it was glad to take what it could get. It was not until the return of more normal conditions that the process of elimination of the incapable and the unfit set in. Meanwhile, in these new fields, the Negro was acquiring all sorts of divergent reputations for capability. In some places he was rated A 1 and in others N. G., and in varying degrees between these two extremes. The explanation, of course, is that different places had secured different kinds of Negroes. On the whole, New York was more fortunate in the migrants she got than were some of the large cities. Most of the industries in the manufacturing cities of the Middle West—except the steel mills, which drew largely on the skilled and semi-skilled labour from the mills of Alabama and Tennessee—received migrants from the cotton-raising regions of the lower Mississippi Valley, from the rural, even the backwoods, districts, Negroes who were unused to city life or anything bearing a resemblance to modern industry. On the other hand, New York drew most of her migrants from cities and towns of the Atlantic seaboard states, Negroes who were far better prepared to adapt themselves to life and industry in a great city. Nor did all of New York's Negro migrants come from the South. The opportunity for Negro labour exerted a pull that reached down to the Negroes of the West Indies, and many of them came, most of them directly to New York. Those from the British West Indies average high in intelligence and efficiency. There is practically no illiteracy among them, and many have a sound English common school education. They are characteristically sober-minded and have something of a genius for business, differing almost totally, in these respects, from the average rural Negro of the South. Those from the British possessions constitute the great majority of the West Indians in New York; but there is also a large number who are Spanish-speaking and a considerable, though smaller, number who are French-speaking. The total West Indian population of Harlem is approximately fifty thousand.

With thousands of Negroes pouring into Harlem month by month, two things happened: first, a sheer physical pressure for room was set up that was irresistible; second, old residents and newcomers got work as fast as they could take it, at wages never dreamed of, so there was now plenty of money for renting and buying. And the Negro in Harlem did, contrary to all the burlesque notions about what Negroes do when they get hold of money, take advantage of the low prices of property and begin to buy. Buying property became a contagious fever. It became a part of the gospel preached in the churches. It seems that generations of the experience of an extremely precarious foothold on the land of Manhattan Island flared up into a conscious determination never to let that condition return. So they turned the money from their new-found prosperity into property. All classes bought. It was not an unknown thing for a coloured washerwoman to walk into a real-estate office and lay down several thousand dollars on a house. There was Mrs. Mary Dean, known as "Pig Foot Mary" because of her high reputation in the business of preparing and selling that particular delicacy, so popular in Harlem. She paid $42,000 for a five-story apartment house at the corner of Seventh Avenue and One Hundred and Thirty-seventh Street, which was sold later to a coloured undertaker for $72,000. The Equitable Life Assurance Company held vacant for quite a while a block of 106 model private houses, designed by Stanford White, which the company had been obliged to take over following the hegira of the whites from Harlem. When they were put on the market, they were promptly bought by Negroes at an aggregate price of about two million dollars. John E. Nail, a coloured real-estate dealer of Harlem who is a member of the Real Estate Board of New York and an appraisal authority, states that Negroes own and control Harlem real property worth, at a conservative estimate, between fifty and sixty million dollars. Relatively, these figures are amazing. Twenty years ago barely a half-dozen coloured individuals owned land on Manhattan. Down to fifteen years ago the amount that Negroes had acquired in Harlem was by comparison negligible. Today a very large part of the property in Harlem occupied by Negroes is owned by Negroes.

It should be noted that Harlem was taken over without violence. In some of the large Northern cities where the same sort of expansion of the Negro population was going on, there was not only strong antagonism on the part of whites, but physical expression of it. In Chicago, Cleveland, and other cities houses bought and moved into by Negroes were bombed. In Chicago a church bought by a coloured congregation was badly damaged by bombs. In other cities several formerly white churches which had been taken over by coloured congregations were bombed. In Detroit, mobs undertook to evict Negroes from houses bought by them in white neighbourhoods. The mob drove vans up to one house just purchased and moved into by a coloured physician, ordered him out, loaded all his goods into the vans, and carted them back to his old residence. These arrogated functions of the mob reached a climax in the celebrated Sweet case. A mob gathered in the evening round a house in a white neighbourhood which Dr. O. H. Sweet, a coloured physician, had bought and moved into the day before. When the situation reached a critical point, shots fired from within the house killed one person in the crowd and seriously wounded another. Dr. Sweet, his wife, and eight others, relatives and friends, who were in the house at the time, were indicted and tried for murder in the first degree. They were defended in two long trials by the National Association for the Advancement of Colored People, through Clarence Darrow and Arthur Garfield Hays, assisted by several local attorneys, and were acquitted. This was the tragic end of eviction by mob in Detroit.

Although there was bitter feeling in Harlem during the fifteen years of struggle the Negro went through in getting a foothold on the land, there was never any demonstration of violence that could be called serious. Not since the riot of 1900 has New York witnessed, except for minor incidents, any interracial disturbances. Not even in the memorable summer of 1919—that summer when the stoutest-hearted Negroes felt terror and dismay; when the race got the worst backwash of the war, and the Ku Klux Klan was in the ascendant; when almost simultaneously there were riots in Chicago and in Longview, Texas; in Omaha and in Phillips County, Arkansas; and hundreds of Negroes, chased through the streets or hunted down through the swamps, were beaten and killed; when in the national capital an anti-Negro mob held sway for three days, in which time six persons were killed and scores severely beaten—not even during this period of massacre did New York, with more than a hundred thousand Negroes grouped together in Harlem, lose its equanimity.

It is apparent that race friction, as it affects Harlem as a community, has grown less and less each year for the past ten years; and the signs are that there will not be a recrudescence. The signs are confirmed by certain basic conditions. Although Harlem is a Negro community, the newest comers do not long remain merely "Harlem Negroes"; astonishingly soon they become New Yorkers. One reason for this is that, by comparison with Chicago, Detroit, Pittsburgh, or Cleveland, there is no gang labour among Negroes in New York. The longshoremen are an exception, but the Negro longshoremen are highly unionized and stand on an equal footing with their white fellow-workers. Employment of Negroes in New York is diversified; they are employed more as individuals than as non-integral parts of a gang. This gives them the opportunity for more intimate contacts with the life and spirit of the city as a whole. A thousand Negroes from Mississippi brought up and put to work in a Pittsburgh plant will for a long time remain a thousand Negroes from Mississippi. Under the conditions that prevail in New York, they would all, inside of six months, be pretty good New Yorkers. One of the chief factors in the Chicago race riot in 1919 was the fact that at the time more than twelve thousand Negroes were employed at the stockyards. Moreover, there is the psychology of New York, the natural psychology of a truly cosmopolitan city, in which there is always the tendency to minimize rather than magnify distinctions of this sort, in which such distinctions tend to die out, unless kept alive by some intentional agency. New York, more than any other American city, maintains a matter-of-fact, a taken-for-granted attitude towards her Negro citizens. Less there than anywhere else in the country are Negroes regarded as occupying a position of wardship; more nearly do they stand upon the footing of common and equal citizenship. It may be that one of the causes of New York's attitude lies in the fact that the Negro there has achieved a large degree of political independence; that he has broken away from a political creed based merely upon traditional and sentimental grounds. Yet, on the other hand, this itself may be a result of New York's attitude.

At any rate, there is no longer any apparent feeling against the occupancy of Harlem by Negroes. Within the past five years the colony has expanded to the south, the north, and the west. It has gone down Seventh Avenue from One Hundred and Twenty-seventh Street to

Central Park at One Hundred and Tenth Street. It has climbed upwards between Eighth Avenue and the Harlem River from One Hundred and Forty-fifth Street to One Hundred and Fifty-fifth. It has spread to the west and occupies the heights of Coogan's Bluff, overlooking Colonial Park. And to the east and west of this solid Negro area, there is a fringe where the population is mixed, white and coloured. This expansion of the past five years has taken place without any physical opposition, or even any considerable outbreak of antagonistic public sentiment.

The question inevitably arises: Will the Negroes of Harlem be able to hold it? Will they not be driven still farther northward? Residents of Manhattan, regardless of race, have been driven out when they lay in the path of business and greatly increased land values. Harlem lies in the direction that path must take; so there is little probability that Negroes will always hold it as a residential section. But this is to be considered: the Negro's situation in Harlem is without precedent in all his history in New York; never before has he been so securely anchored, never before has he owned the land, never before has he had so well established a community life. It is probable that land through the heart of Harlem will some day so increase in value that Negroes may not be able to hold it—although it is quite as probable that there will be some Negroes able to take full advantage of the increased values—and will be forced to make a move. But the next move, when it comes, will be unlike the others. It will not be a move made solely at the behest of someone else; it will be more in the nature of a bargain. Nor will it be a move in which the Negro will carry with him only his household goods and utensils; he will move at a financial profit to himself. But at the present time such a move is nowhere in sight.

FOURTEEN

WITHIN THE PAST TEN YEARS HARLEM has acquired a worldwide reputation. It has gained a place in the list of famous sections of great cities. It is known in Europe and the Orient, and it is talked about by natives in the interior of Africa. It is farthest known as being exotic, colourful, and sensuous; a place of laughing, singing, and dancing; a place where life wakes up at night. This phase of Harlem's fame is most widely known because, in addition to being spread by ordinary agencies, it has been proclaimed in story and song. And certainly this is Harlem's most striking and fascinating aspect. New Yorkers and people visiting New York from the world over go to the night-clubs of Harlem and dance to such jazz music as can be heard nowhere else; and they get an exhilaration impossible to duplicate. Some of these seekers after new sensations go beyond the gay night-clubs; they peep in under the more seamy side of things; they nose down into lower strata of life. A visit to Harlem at night—the principal streets never deserted, gay crowds skipping from one place of amusement to another, lines of taxicabs and limousines standing under the sparkling lights of the entrances to the famous night-clubs, the subway kiosks swallowing and disgorging crowds all night long—gives the impression that Harlem never sleeps and that the inhabitants thereof jazz through existence. But, of course, no one can seriously think that the two hundred thousand and more Negroes in Harlem spend their nights on any such pleasance. Of a necessity the vast majority of them are ordinary, hard-working people, who spend their time in just about the same way that other ordinary, hard-working people do. Most of them have never seen the inside of a nightclub. The great bulk of them are confronted with the stern necessity of making a living, of making both ends meet, of finding money to pay the rent and keep the children fed and clothed neatly enough to attend school; their waking hours are almost entirely consumed in this unromantic task. And it is a task in which they cannot escape running up against a barrier erected especially for them, a barrier which pens them off on the morass—no, the quicksands—of economic insecurity. Fewer jobs are open to them than to any other group; and in such jobs as they get, they are subject to the old rule, which still obtains, "the last to be hired and the first to be fired."

Notwithstanding all that, gaiety is peculiarly characteristic of Harlem. The people who live there are by nature a pleasure-loving people; and though most of them must take their pleasures in a less expensive manner than in nightly visits to clubs, they nevertheless, as far as they can afford—and often much farther—do satisfy their hunger for enjoyment. And since they are constituted as they are, enjoyment being almost as essential to them as food, perhaps really a compensation which enables them to persist, it is well that they are able to extract pleasure easily and cheaply. An average group of Negroes can in dancing to a good jazz band achieve a delightful state of intoxication that for others would require nothing short of a certain per capita imbibition of synthetic gin. The masses of Harlem get a good deal of pleasure out of things far too simple for most other folks. In the evenings of summer and on Sundays they get lots of enjoyment out of strolling.

Strolling is almost a lost art in New York; at least, in the manner in which it is so generally practised in Harlem. Strolling in Harlem does not mean merely walking along Lenox or upper Seventh Avenue or One Hundred and Thirty-fifth Street; it means that those streets are places for socializing. One puts on one's best clothes and fares forth to pass the time pleasantly with the friends and acquaintances and, most important of all, the strangers he is sure of meeting. One saunters along, he hails this one, exchanges a word or two with that one, stops for a short chat with the other one. He comes up to a laughing, chattering group, in which he may have only one friend or acquaintance, but that gives him the privilege of joining in. He does join in and takes part in the joking, the small talk and gossip, and makes new acquaintances. He passes on and arrives in front of one of the theatres, studies the bill for a while, undecided about going in. He finally moves on a few steps farther and joins another group and is introduced to two or three pretty girls who have just come to Harlem, perhaps only for a visit; and finds a reason to be glad that he postponed going into the theatre. The hours of a summer evening run by rapidly. This is not simply going out for a walk; it is more like going out for adventure.

In almost as simple a fashion the masses of Harlem get enjoyment out of church-going. This enjoyment, however, is not quite so inexpensive as strolling can be made. Some critics of the Negro—especially Negro critics—say that religion costs him too much; that he has too many churches, and that many of them are magnificent beyond his means; that church mortgages and salaries and upkeep consume the greater part of the financial margin of the race and keep its economic nose to the grindstone. All of which is, in the main, true. There are something like one hundred and sixty coloured churches in Harlem. A hundred of these could be closed and there would be left a sufficient number to supply the religious needs of the community. There would be left, in fact, just about the number of churches that are regularly organized and systematically administered and that could be adequately supported. The superfluous one hundred or more are ephemeral and nomadic, belonging to no established denomination and within no classification. They are here today and gone somewhere else or gone entirely tomorrow. They are housed in rented quarters, a store, the floor of a private dwelling, or even the large room of a flat; and remain as long as the rent can be met or until a move is made, perhaps, to other quarters. Doubtless some of the founders of these excess churches are sincere, though ignorant; but it is certain that many of them are parasitical fakers, even downright scoundrels, who count themselves successful when they have under the guise of religion got enough hard-working women together to ensure them an easy living. This little-church movement has also given rise to many cults and much occultism. Ira De A. Reid, of the National Urban League, recently made a survey of the churches of Harlem and found that there had been a rapid growth in the number of religious sects that studied and practised esoteric mysteries. In his report he says: "There are they who dabble in spiritualism, exhibiting their many charms and wares in the form of Grand Imperial incense, prayer incense, aluminum trumpets, luminous bands and other accessories." Among these cults some of the names found by Mr. Reid were: the Commandment Keepers, Holy Church of the Living God, the Pillar and Ground of Truth, the Temple of the Gospel of the Kingdom, the Metaphysical Church of the Divine Investigation, Prophet Bess, St. Matthew's Church of the Divine Silence and Truth, Tabernacle of the Congregation of the Disciples of the Kingdom, the Church of the Temple of Love. Taking the situation as a whole, there is truly a wide margin of money, effort, and energy that could be saved or more effectively spent by cutting out all extravagances in the needed churches, cutting off the waste brought about by the needless churches, and abolishing entirely the bootleggers of religion.

The multiplicity of churches in Harlem, and in every other Negro community, is commonly accounted for by the innate and deep religious emotion of the race. Conceding the strength and depth of this emotion, there is also the vital fact that coloured churches provide their members with a great deal of enjoyment, aside from the joys of religion. Indeed, a Negro church is for its members much more besides a place of worship. It is a social centre, it is a club, it is an arena for the exercise of one's capabilities and powers, a world in which one may achieve self-realization and preferment. Of course, a church means something of the same sort to all groups; but with the Negro all these attributes are magnified because of the fact that they are so curtailed for him in the world at large. Most of the large Harlem churches open early on Sunday morning and remain open until ten or eleven o'clock at night; and there is not an hour during that time when any one of them is empty. A good many people stay in church all day; there they take their dinner, cooked and served hot by a special committee. Aside from any spiritual benefits derived, going to church means being dressed in one's best clothes, forgetting for the time about work, having the chance to acquit oneself with credit before one's fellows, and having the opportunity of meeting, talking, and laughing with friends and of casting an appraising and approving eye upon the opposite sex. Going to church is an outlet for the Negro's religious emotions; but not the least reason why he is willing to support so many churches is that they furnish so many agreeable activities and so much real enjoyment. He is willing to support them because he has not yet, and will not have until there is far greater economic and intellectual development and social organization, any other agencies that can fill their place.

The importance of the place of the church in Negro life is not comparable with its importance among other American groups. In a community like Harlem, which has not yet attained cohesion and adjustment, the church is a stabilizing force. The integrating value of the churches in Harlem, where there are so many disintegrating forces at work, can easily be underestimated. This is especially true of churches like Mother Zion, St. Philip's, and Abyssinian, each of which is an organization with over a hundred years of continuous historical background. The severest critic of the shortcomings of the Negro church would pause before wishing a Harlem without churches. What intelligent criticism should at present insist upon is that the Negro church live more fully up to the responsibilities and opportunities which it has over and above those of the churches of other groups; that it throw out moss-back theology and obsolete dogmatics and strive to make itself a greater force in bettering the Negro's state in this world and in this country; that it seek to give out larger and larger essential values in return for the millions of dollars the Negro masses pour into its coffers. There is not now any other piece of organization machinery that could do these things as well as the Negro church could do them. In so doing, the church would not limit, but would extend, its spiritual forces. Much higher spiritual returns could be gained by explanations to the masses of the economic factors involved in the condition of the race than by inane fulminations against dancing and theatre-going. Some ministers meet criticism of this sort by asking the critics why they do not complain as loudly about the money that Negroes spend in places of amusement as they do about the money Negroes give to the church. That is a sound question as far as it goes, but it does not go all the way. No one who spends money in a cabaret, for instance, has any right to demand of the proprietor of the place what use he proposes to make of that money; on the other hand, the church is a corporate membership institution, and those who give to its support have every right to ask about the administration of its resources. But outside criticism, however intelligent, won't go very far towards changing things; it is possible for it to have just the opposite effect; the change must be wrought from within. And it may be that there will rise up out of that element of the coloured clergy which realizes the potentialities of a modern Negro Church a man with sufficient wisdom and power to bring about a new Reformation.

In Harlem, as in all American Negro communities, the fraternal bodies also fill an important place. These fraternities, too, are in a very large degree social organizations, but they have also an economic feature. In addition to providing the enjoyment of lodge meetings, lodge balls and picnics, and the interest and excitement of lodge politics, there are provisions for taking care of the sick and burying the dead. Both of these latter provisions are highly commendable and are the means of attracting a good many members; however, the criticism can be made that very often the amount of money spent for burying the dead is out of proportion to that spent in caring for the living. Indeed, this is so general that it makes "the high cost of dying" a live question among Negroes.

Harlem is also a parade ground. During the warmer months of the year no Sunday passes without several parades. There are brass bands, marchers in resplendent regalia, and high dignitaries with gorgeous insignia riding in automobiles. Almost any excuse for parading is sufficient—the funeral of a member of the lodge, the laying of a cornerstone, the annual sermon to the order, or just a general desire to "turn out." Parades are not limited to Sundays; for when the funeral of a lodge member falls on a weekday, it is quite the usual thing to hold the exercises at night, so that members of the order and friends who are at work during the day may attend. Frequently after nightfall a slow procession may be seen wending its way along and a band heard playing a dirge that takes on a deeply sepulchral tone. But generally these parades are lively and add greatly to the movement, colour, and gaiety of Harlem. A brilliant parade with very good bands is participated in not only by the marchers in line, but also by the marchers on the sidewalks. For it is not a universal custom of Harlem to stand idly and watch a parade go by; a good part of the crowd always marches along, keeping step to the music.

Now, it would be entirely misleading to create the impression that all Harlem indulges in none other than these Arcadian-like pleasures. There is a large element of educated, well-to-do metropolitans among the Negroes of Harlem who view with indulgence, often with something less, the responses of the masses to these artless amusements. There is the solid, respectable, bourgeois class, of the average proportion, whose counterpart is to be found in every Southern city. There are strictly social sets that go in for bridge parties, breakfast parties, cocktail parties, for high-powered cars, weekends, and exclusive dances. Occasionally an exclusive dance is held in one of the ballrooms of a big downtown hotel. Harlem has its sophisticated, fast sets, initiates in all the wisdom of worldliness. And Harlem has, too, its underworld, its world of pimps and prostitutes, of gamblers and thieves, of illicit love and illicit liquor, of red sins and dark crimes. In a word, Harlem possesses in some degree all of the elements of a cosmopolitan centre. And by that same word, striking an average, we find that the overwhelming majority of its people are people whose counterparts may be found in any American community. Yet as a whole community it possesses a sense of humour and a love of gaiety that are distinctly characteristic.

FIFTEEN

D URING THE TERM OF EXILE OF the Negro from the downtown
    theatres of New York, which began in 1910 and lasted for seven
lean years, there grew up in Harlem a real Negro theatre, something New
York had never had before; that is, a theatre in which Negro performers
played to audiences made up almost wholly of people of their own race.
In several Southern cities there had been for a decade or more theatres
where the audiences, on account of the laws separating the races in places
of amusement, were strictly coloured. And in Chicago there was the Pekin
Theatre, a Negro theatre patronized principally by coloured people. But
the professional experience of Negro performers in New York had always
been to play before audiences predominantly white. The rise of a Negro
theatre in Harlem was, therefore, a new thing; and, because it was within
the radius of the circle in which the theatrical forces of the country are
centred, it proved to be a very important thing. It is not an exaggeration to
say that it worked some vital changes. The Negro performer in New York,
who had always been playing to white or predominantly white audiences,
found himself in an entirely different psychological atmosphere. He found
himself freed from a great many restraints and taboos that had cramped
him for forty years. In all those years he had been constrained to do a
good many things that were distasteful because managers felt they were

things that would please white folks. Likewise he was forbidden to do some other things because managers feared they would displease white folks. One of the well-known taboos was that there should never be any romantic love-making in a Negro play. If anything approaching a love duet was introduced in a musical comedy, it had to be broadly burlesqued. The reason behind this taboo lay in the belief that a love scene between two Negroes could not strike a white audience except as ridiculous. The taboo existed in deference to the superiority stereotype that Negroes cannot be supposed to mate romantically, but do so in some sort of minstrel fashion or in some more primeval manner than white people. This taboo had been one of the most strictly observed. In the middle theatrical period Cole and Johnson had come nearest to breaking it in their *Shoofly Regiment* and *Red Moon*. Williams and Walker never seriously attempted to do so. So, with the establishment of the Negro theatre in Harlem, coloured performers in New York experienced for the first time release from the restraining fears of what a white audience would stand for; for the first time they felt free to do on the stage whatever they were able to do.

This sense of freedom manifested itself in efforts covering a wide range; efforts that ran all the way from crude Negro burlesque to Broadway drama. This intermediate and experimental theatrical period developed mainly in two Harlem theatres, the Lafayette and the Lincoln. Within several years both these houses had good stock-companies, and for quite a while their repertories consisted chiefly of downtown successes. The Lafayette Players developed into a very proficient organization that gave adequate presentations of *Madame X, The Servant in the House, On Trial, The Love of Choo Chin, Within the Law,* and other such plays. These melodramatic plays made a great appeal to Harlem audiences. To most of the people that crowded the Lafayette and the Lincoln the thrill received from these pieces was an entirely new experience; and it was all the closer and more moving because it was expressed in terms of their own race. For a time Negro sketches and musical shows were swept off the stage, but they are now back again.

The two stock-companies had as members some performers who came down from the days of the Isham, Williams and Walker, Cole and Johnson shows; and they also developed a number of young dramatic actors who became great Harlem favourites. There were Anita Bush, Inez Clough, Abbie Mitchell, Ida Anderson, Evelyn Ellis, Lottie Grady, Laura Bowman, Susie Sutton, Cleo Desmond, Edna Thomas, Charles Gilpin, Frank Wilson, Tom Brown, Charles Moore, Sidney Kirkpatrick, Lionel Monagas, A. B. Comathiere, Walter Thompson, "Babe" Townsend, Charles Olden, Andrew Bishop, Clarence Muse, Jack Carter. All of these names were as well known to Harlem as those of Broadway favourites to the rest of the city. Readers who are at all familiar with the present period of the Negro in the theatre will see that in this list there are those who did not remain limited to Harlem or to the circuit played by the Harlem stock-companies, but helped to place the Negro fairly and squarely on Broadway. The Negro theatre in Harlem, in which the coloured performer gained a new freedom and new incentives, proved to be the exact medium he needed through which to fit himself for the fresh start he was to make.

All through this intermediate period there were times when polite comedy and high-tension melodrama gave way to black-face farce, hilarious musical comedy, and bills of specialties. The black Harlem audiences enjoyed being thrilled, but they also wanted to laugh. And a Negro audience seems never to laugh heartier than when laughing at itself—provided it is a *strictly* Negro audience. There were several Negro producers who kept the older tradition alive: the Tutt brothers—Whitney and J. Homer—Irving C. Miller, and S. H. Dudley. Their productions always drew good houses. But in this field there stands out above them all a musical show produced at the Lafayette Theatre in 1913, which not only played to great local crowds, but brought Broadway up to Harlem. The piece was *Darktown Follies*, written and staged by Leubrie Hill, formerly a member of the Williams and Walker company. *Darktown Follies* drew space, headlines, and cartoons in the New York papers; and consequently it became the vogue to go to Harlem to see it. This was the beginning of the nightly migration to Harlem in search of entertainment. One visitor to the *Darktown Follies* was Florenz Ziegfeld, and a very much interested visitor he was. He bought the rights to produce the finale to the first act and several song numbers in his own *Follies*. The finale to the first act of *Darktown Follies* was one of those miracles of originality which occasionally come to pass in the world of musical comedy. Its title was "At the Ball," the tune was the sort of melody that, once heard, is unforgettable, and words and music were combined into a very clever piece of syncopation. But it was the staging that made it so striking. The whole company formed an endless chain that passed before the footlights and behind the scenes, round and round, singing and executing a movement from a dance called "ballin' the jack," one of those Negro dances which periodically come along and sweep the country. This finale was one of the greatest hits the *Ziegfeld Follies* ever had. One of the song numbers Mr. Ziegfeld took was "Rock Me in the Cradle of Love," which in the *Darktown Follies* had been sung by the Negro tenor to the bronze soubrette in a most impassioned manner, demonstrating that the love-making taboo had been absolutely kicked out of the Negro theatre. In 1915 Edward Sterling Wright came to the Lafayette Theatre with a very creditable presentation of *Othello*.

This period in Harlem filled in the gap between the second and third periods of the Negro in the theatre. The third period is now in full swing, and the Negro theatre in Harlem is also very much alive. At present, aside from the picture houses, there are three large Negro theatres in Harlem. The third was added when several years ago the Alhambra Theatre on Seventh Avenue near One Hundred and Twenty-fifth Street, long a Keith vaudeville house, was converted into a theatre for performances given by and for Negroes.

April 5, 1917 is the date of the most important single event in the entire history of the Negro in the American theatre; for it marks the beginning of a new era. On that date a performance of three dramatic plays was given by the Coloured Players at the Garden Theatre in Madison Square Garden, New York, and the stereotyped traditions regarding the Negro's histrionic limitations were smashed. It was the first time anywhere in the United States for Negro actors in the dramatic theatre to command the serious attention of the critics and of the general press and public.

The plays were three one-act plays written by Ridgely Torrence; they were produced by Mrs. Emily Hapgood; the settings and costumes were designed by Robert Edmond Jones, and the staging was under his direction. The acting was fine; in several of the roles it was superb. In fact, nothing that has been done since has afforded Negro performers such a wide gamut for their powers. The praise of the critics was enthusiastic and practically unanimous.

The performance opened with *The Rider of Dreams*, a play of rustic Negro life, and a true comedy. The second play was *Granny Maumee*, a tragedy of the colour-line, which contained a vivid scene of voodoo enchantment. The play that closed the performance was *Simon the Cyrenian*, which was billed as "A Passion Interlude." It was the story of

Simon, the black man who was Jesus' cross-bearer.

The casts of the three plays were:

The Rider of Dreams A Comedy Cast of Characters

Lucy Sparrow...............Blanche Deas

Booker Sparrow..............Joseph Burt

Madison Sparrow..............Opal Cooper

Dr. Williams..............Alexander Rogers

Granny Maumee A Tragedy Cast of Characters

Granny Maumee..............Marie Jackson Sturat

Pearl..............Fannie Tarkington

Sapphie..............Blanche Deas

Simon the Cyrenian A Passion Interlude

"And as they led Him away, they laid hold upon one Simon, a Cyrenian . . . and on him they laid the cross, that he might bear it after Jesus." Luke xxiii, 26.

Cast of Characters

Procula..............Inez Clough

Drusus..............Andrew Bishop

Acte, Princess of Egypt..............Lottie Grady

Battus..............Theodore Roosevelt Bolin

Simon..............John T. Butler

Pilate..............Alexander Rogers

Barabbas..............Jesse Shipp

The Mocker with the Crown of Thorns..............Robert Atkin

The Mocker with the Scarlet Robe..............Thomas William

Egyptian Herald..............Frederick Slade

Centurion..............Jerome Osborne, Jr.

Longinus...............Ralph Hernandez

Jervis Wilson

Soldiers...............Earl Taylor

Lisle Berridge

Attendants to Procula..............Thomas William

(Muriel Smith)

Scene: The Garden of Pilate's House at Jerusalem.

Time: The day of Jesus' Crucifixion.

These plays, a rustic comedy, a voodoo tragedy, and the passion interlude, made a high demand on the versatility of the company: the first called for humorous characterization, the second for dramatic power, and the third for finished acting. The demand was fully measured up to. George Jean Nathan, in making his estimate of the ten most distinguished performers of the year, gave Opal Cooper for his work in *The Rider of Dreams* seventh place in the list of male actors, and Inez Clough for her portrayal of Procula, the wife of Pilate, in *Simon the Cyrenian*, ninth place among the women.

A glance at the casts of these plays will show some names that have by now become a bit familiar to the reader, and will also buttress the statement made earlier in this book that the accumulation of theatrical training and stage technique has made possible the higher development of each period of the Negro in the theatre over the period preceding. This knocks something of a hole in the popular idea that Negroes, because of their marked aptitude for the theatre, simply walk out on the stage and act. In certain exceptional cases they do, but generally they do not. We see the name of Jesse Shipp. Mr. Shipp's professional experience goes back to the minstrel period, with Primrose and West's "Forty Whites and Thirty Blacks," and comes down through the Isham, the Cole and Johnson, and the Williams and Walker shows. At the present time Mr. Shipp is playing a part in *The Green Pastures*. Alex Rogers came down through the Williams and Walker shows. Miss Clough came down through the Isham and the Cole and Johnson shows and the Lafayette Players. Miss Deas came through the Cole and Johnson shows. In addition to Miss Clough, the Lafayette Players were represented by Andrew Bishop and Lottie Grady. One of those special exceptions was Opal Cooper. Mr. Cooper had never been on the professional stage before; his sole previous preparation was what he had gained as an entertainer in a night-club. John T. Butler, who played the role of Simon, was a post-office employee and had acquired his experience in amateur and semi-professional theatricals. Marie Jackson Stuart had long been a dramatic reader.

A notable feature of the production was the singing orchestra under the direction of J. Rosamond Johnson. A singing orchestra as part of a play was at the time a distinct innovation in the theatre in New York. The Coloured Players remained ten days at the Garden Theatre, then moved up to the Garrick with every promise of success; but the fates planned otherwise. The Coloured Players opened on April 5, 1917; and on the following day, April 6, the United States declared war against the Imperial German Government. They played at the Garrick for several weeks, but the increasing stress of the war was too great, even for stronger enterprises in the theatre, and it crushed them out. Nevertheless, this effort marked the beginning of the third, and present, period of the Negro in the American theatre. And it was Emily Hapgood, who has recently died, who first demonstrated the faith that the Negro could make a place on the legitimate stage. After the close of the war the effort was carried forward.

In addition to the theatre in Harlem, there has been another medium through which significant effect has been wrought on the Negro in the theatre; that medium is the night-clubs. To many, especially among coloured people, a Harlem night-club is a den of iniquity, where the Devil holds high revel. The fact is that the average night-club is as orderly as many a Sunday-school picnic has been. These clubs are patronized by many quite respectable citizens. Anyone who visits them expecting to be shocked is likely to be disappointed. Generally night-clubbers go simply to have a good time. They laugh and talk and they dance to the most exhilarating music. And they watch a first-rate revue. Certainly, there are infractions of the Volstead Act; but they also take place in the best-regulated homes. The larger clubs maintain permanent companies of performers; and such clubs as Connie's Inn, the Cotton Club, and Small's Paradise put on revues that are often better than what may be seen in the theatres downtown. The night-clubs have been the training ground for a good part of the talent that has been drawn upon by musical comedy and revues in the professional theatre; and not only for strictly Negro productions, but also for productions in which there have been mixed casts, as, for example, in *Show Boat* and *Golden Dawn*.

The night-clubs also constitute the stage for a number of crack Negro bands. Duke Ellington's is one of the most famous jazz bands in the country. Fletcher Henderson's is another, which, however, generally plays in a downtown club. There are hundreds of musicians and hundreds of performers connected with the night-clubs of Harlem. The waiters, cooks, coat-room girls, doormen and others make up several more hundreds. It has been estimated that there are something like two thousand Negroes employed in these clubs.

The little-theatre movement has also been started and restarted in

Harlem, as the various efforts for establishment flourished and died. There have been three or four definite and partially successful efforts. The most successful was made by the Krigwa Players, organized by W. E. Burghardt Du Bois in connexion with the literary and artistic program of the *Crisis* magazine. The Krigwa Players had the distinction of winning a place in the Little Theatre Tournament, 1927, to compete for the David Belasco trophy. The company did not win the trophy, but its play, *The Fool's Errand*, written by Eulalie Spence, a New York coloured girl, was awarded one of the Samuel French prizes for the best unpublished manuscript plays in the contest.

SIXTEEN

O N DECEMBER 15, 1919 JOHN DRINKWATER'S *Abraham Lincoln* had its American premiere at the Cort Theatre in New York, and Charles Gilpin, formerly with both the Lincoln and the Lafayette companies, was drafted to create the role of the Rev. William Custis, a Negro preacher who goes to the White House for a conference at the request of Lincoln, this conference between the President and the black man constituting one of the strongest and most touching scenes in the play. The character of Custis was intended by the playwright to be a representation of Frederick Douglass. Drinkwater in writing the play had largely followed Lord Charnwood's life of Abraham Lincoln, in which Douglass is erroneously set down as "a well-known Negro preacher." The playwright also made the error of putting Custis's lines into dialect. He may, as a dramatist, have done this intentionally to heighten the character effect; or he may, as an Englishman, have done it through unfamiliarity with all the facts. In either case, the dialect was such as no American Negro would ever use. It was a slightly darkened pidgin-English or the form of speech a big Indian chief would be supposed to employ in talking with the Great White Father at Washington. However, Gilpin was a success in the role.

Meanwhile Eugene O'Neill was experimenting with the dramatic possibilities of the Negro both as material and as exponent. He had written a one-act play, *The Moon of the Caribbees*, in which the scene was laid aboard a ship lying in a West Indian harbour, and the characters were members of the ship's crew and Negro natives of the island. The play was produced at the Provincetown Playhouse, New York, in 1918, with a white cast. He had also written a one-act tragedy, *The Dreamy Kid*, in which all of the four characters were Negroes. *The Dreamy Kid* was produced at the Provincetown Playhouse, October 31, 1919, with a Negro cast and with Harold Simmelkjaer—who, despite the Dutch name, is a Negro—in the title role. This play was later revived with Frank Wilson as the Dreamy Kid. In the season of 1919–20 Butler Davenport's Bramhall Players produced at their playhouse in East Twenty-seventh Street a play called *Justice* with a mixed cast. Frank Wilson and Rose McClendon played important parts.

None of these efforts, so far as the Negro is concerned, evoked more than mildly favourable comment. But on November 3, 1920 O'Neill's *The Emperor Jones* was produced at the Provincetown Playhouse, with Charles Gilpin in the title role, and another important page in the history of the Negro in the theatre was written. The next morning Gilpin was famous. The power of his acting was enthusiastically and universally acclaimed. Indeed, the sheer physical feat of sustaining the part—the whole play is scarcely more than a continuous monologue spoken by the principal character—demanded admiration. The Drama League voted him to be one of the ten persons who had done most for the American theatre during the year; and some of the readers of these pages will recall the almost national crisis that was brought on as a consequence of this action.

As was the custom, the Drama League gave a dinner in honour of the ten persons chosen; and, as seemed quite natural to do, invited Mr. Gilpin. Thereupon there broke out a controversy that divided the Drama League, the theatrical profession, the press, and the public. Pressure was brought to have the invitation withdrawn, but those responsible for it stood firm. Then the pressure was centred upon Mr. Gilpin to induce him not to attend the dinner. The amount of noise and heat made, and of serious effort expended, was worthy of a weightier matter than the question of a dinner with a coloured man present as a guest. This incident occurred only ten years ago, but already it has an archaic character. It is doubtful if a similar incident today could provoke such a degree of asininity. Mr. Gilpin attended the dinner.

By his work in *The Emperor Jones* Gilpin reached the highest point of achievement on the legitimate stage that had yet been attained by a Negro in America. But it was by no sudden flight; it was by a long, hard struggle. Before being dined by the Drama League as one of those who had done most for the American theatre, he had travelled with small road shows playing one-night stands, been stranded more than once, been compelled to go back to work at his trade as a printer, been a member of a minstrel show, worked in a barber-shop, joined a street fair company, gone out with a concert company, tried being a trainer of prize-fighters, sung with a company of jubilee singers, worked as an elevator-boy and switchboard operator in an apartment house on Riverside Drive, been a railroad porter, played vaudeville, held a job as a janitor, and hesitated greatly about giving it up. His real theatrical career can be traced from Williams and Walker's company to Gus Hill's *Smart Set*, to the Pekin stock-company, to the Anita Bush Players at the Lincoln in Harlem, to the Lafayette Players, to John Drinkwater's *Abraham Lincoln*, and to *The Emperor Jones*. Mr. Gilpin was awarded the Spingarn Medal[1] in 1920. He died May 6, 1930.

Torrence and O'Neill were not the only playwrights of these latter days to experiment with the Negro as a theme for the theatre, but they were the first to use the Negro and Negro life as pure dramatic material. In 1905 there was produced at the Amsterdam Theatre (New York) *The Clansman* by the Rev. Thomas Dixon. This play was a rehash of the animosities of Reconstruction days, following the Civil War, and an attempt to intensify sentiment against the Negro. In 1909 *The Nigger* by Edward Sheldon was produced at the New Theatre (New York). This play, too, was set in the Reconstruction period, but the situation was viewed from an almost opposite angle. In 1916 Robert Hilliard produced *Pride of Race* at the Maxine Elliott Theatre (New York) and played the leading role. This play was built on that bit of pseudo-science which holds that to a white person and a coloured person whose Negro blood cannot even be discerned there may be born a tar-black baby. These were plays of propaganda; they were played by wholly white casts; for them the Negro was merely thematic material. They did not contemplate him as an exponent.

The following year the Negro came back to the New York theatre in his more familiar role. In the summer of 1921 along came *Shuffle Along*, and all New York flocked to the Sixty-third Street Theatre to hear the most joyous singing and see the most exhilarating dancing to be found on any stage in the city. *Shuffle Along* was a record-breaking,

1. The Spingarn Medal was instituted in 1914 by J. E. Spingarn, treasurer of the National Association for the Advancement of Colored People, and is awarded annually for "the highest or noblest achievement by an American Negro during the preceding year or years."

epoch- making musical comedy. Some of its tunes—"I'm Just Wild about Harry," "Gipsy Blues," "Love Will Find a Way," "I'm Cravin' for That Kind of Love," "In Honeysuckle Time," "Bandana Days," and "Shuffle Along"—went round the world. It would be difficult to name another musical comedy with so many song hits as *Shuffle Along* had. Its dances furnished new material for hundreds of dancing perform- ers. *Shuffle Along* was cast in the form of the best Williams and Walker, Cole and Johnson tradition; but the music did not hark back at all; it was up to the minute. There was, however, one other respect in which it did hark back; it was written and produced, as well as performed, by Negroes. Four men—F. E. Miller, Aubrey Lyles, Eubie Blake, and Noble Sissle—combined their talents and their means to bring it about. Their talents were many, but their means were limited, and they had no easy time.

They organized the show in New York and took it on a short out-of- town try-out, with Broadway as their goal. It was booked for an opening at the Howard Theatre, a coloured theatre in Washington. When the company assembled at the Pennsylvania Station, it was found that they did not have quite enough money for transportation, and there had to be quick scurrying round to raise the necessary funds. Such an ominous situation could not well be concealed, and there were misgivings and mutterings among the company. After all the tickets were secured, it took considerable persuasion to induce some of its members to go so far away from New York on such slim expectations.

They played two successful weeks at the Howard Theatre and so had enough money to move to Philadelphia, where they were booked to play the Dunbar Theatre, another coloured house. Broadway, their goal, looked quite distant even from Philadelphia. The managers, seeking to make sure of getting the company to New York, suggested to the owner of the Dunbar Theatre that it would be a good investment for him to take a half-interest in the show for one thousand dollars, but he couldn't see it that way. They played two smashing weeks at the Dunbar and brought the company intact into New York, but, as they expressed it, on a shoe-string. They went into the Sixty-third Street Theatre, which had been dark for some time; it was pretty far uptown for Broadway audiences. Within a few weeks *Shuffle Along* made the Sixty-third Street Theatre one of the best-known houses in town and made it necessary for the Traffic Department to declare Sixty-third Street a one-way thoroughfare. *Shuffle Along* played New York for over a year and played on the road for two years longer. It was a remarkable aggregation. There was a chorus of pretty girls that danced marvellously. The comedians were Miller and Lyles, and a funny blackface pair they were. Their burlesque of two ignorant Negroes going into "big business" and opening a grocery-store was a never-failing producer of side-shaking laughter. There was a quartet, the Four Harmony Kings, that gave a fresh demonstration of the close harmony and barbershop chords that are the chief characteristics of Negro quartets. There was Lottie Gee, jauntiest of *ingenues,* and Gertrude Saunders, most bubbling of comediennes. There was Noble Sissle with his take-it-from-me style of singing, and there was Eubie Blake with his amazing jazz piano-playing. And it was in *Shuffle Along* that Florence Mills, that incomparable little star, first twinkled on Broadway.

Shuffle Along pre-empted and held New York's interest in Negro theatricals for a year. In the fall of 1921 another venture was made, when Irving C. Miller, a brother of the Miller of *Shuffle Along,* produced *Put and Take,* a musical comedy, at Town Hall (New York). *Put and Take,* by all ordinary standards, was a good show, but it was overshadowed by the great vogue of *Shuffle Along.* In the spring of 1923 Irving C. Miller had better success with *Liza*, a tuneful and very fast dancing show that he produced at a downtown theatre.

In the fall Miller and Lyles came out with a new play, *Runnin' Wild*, and opened at the Colonial Theatre, on upper Broadway, on October 29. The old combination had been broken. Miller and Lyles had remained together; Sissle and Blake had formed a separate partnership, and Florence Mills was lost to both sides; she was heading a revue at the Plantation, a downtown night-club. Notwithstanding, *Runnin' Wild*, even in the inevitable comparison with its predecessor, was a splendid show. It had a successful run of eight months at the Colonial. *Runnin' Wild* would have been notable if for no other reason than that it made use of the "Charleston," a Negro dance creation which up to that time had been known only to Negroes; thereby introducing it to New York, America, and the world. The music for the dance was written by Jimmie Johnson, the composer of the musical score of the piece. The Charleston achieved a popularity second only to the tango, also a Negro dance creation, originating in Cuba, transplanted to the Argentine, thence to the world via Paris. There is a claim that Irving C. Miller first introduced the Charleston on the stage in his *Liza*; even so, it was *Runnin' Wild* that started the dance on its world-encircling course. When Miller and Lyles introduced the dance in their show, they did not depend wholly upon their extraordinarily good jazz band for the accompaniment; they went straight back to primitive Negro music and had the major part of the chorus supplement the band by beating out the time with hand-clapping and foot-patting. The effect was electrical. Such a demonstration of beating out complex rhythms had never before been seen on a stage in New York. However, Irving C. Miller may indisputably claim that in his show *Dinah*, produced the next year at the Lafayette Theatre, he was the first to put another Negro dance, the "Black Bottom," on the stage.

The "Black Bottom" gained a popularity which was only little less than that of the Charleston.

The Sissle and Blake show of this same year was *Chocolate Dandies*. In comparison with *Runnin' Wild*, its greatest lack lay in the fact that it had no comedians who approached the class of Miller and Lyles. But *Chocolate Dandies* did have Johnny Hudgins, and in the chorus a girl who showed herself to be a comedienne of the first order. Her name was Josephine Baker.

On May 7, 1923 there was witnessed at the Frazee Theatre what was the most ambitious attempt Negroes had yet made in the legitimate theatre in New York. The Ethiopian Art Players, organized by Raymond O'Neil and Mrs. Sherwood Anderson, presented Oscar Wilde's *Salome*; an original interpretation of Shakspere's *The Comedy of Errors*; and *The Chip Woman's Fortune*, a one-act Negro play by Willis Richardson. The acting of Evelyn Preer in the role of Salome, and her beauty, received high and well-deserved praise from the critics; and the work of Sidney Kirkpatrick, Laura Bowman, Charles Olden, and Lionel Monagas, all formerly of the Lafayette Players, won commendation. But the only play on the bill that was fully approved was *The Chip Woman's Fortune*. Some of the critics said frankly that however well Negroes might play "white" classics like Salome and *The Comedy of Errors*, it was doubtful if they could be so interesting as they would be in Negro plays, if they could be interesting at all. The Ethiopian Art Players had run up against one of the curious factors in the problem of race, against the paradox which makes it quite seemly for a white person to represent a Negro on the stage, but a violation of some inner code for a Negro to represent a white person. This, it seems, is certain: if they had put into a well-written play of Negro life the same degree of talent and skill they did put into *Salome* and *The Comedy of Errors*, they would have achieved an overwhelming success. But it appears that at the time no such play was available for them. Beginning June 4, the company played for a week at the Lafayette in Harlem.

In the same year *Taboo*, a play that had for its theme African voodooism, written by Mary Hoyt Wiborg, a white playwright, was produced at the Sam Harris Theatre (New York). The most important thing about this play was that in it Paul Robeson made his first appearance on the professional stage, playing the role of the voodoo king opposite Margaret Wycherly's voodoo queen. The outstanding feature of the play, however, was an African dance done by C. Kamba Simango, a native, and at the time a student at Columbia University. *Taboo*, after a brief run, was taken to London, where it was better received than in New York. Robeson went to London and acted his same role, playing opposite to Mrs. Patrick Campbell. 1923 also saw the production of *Roseanne*, a play of Negro life in the South, having to do with a transgressing preacher and his, finally, avenging congregation. The play, like *Taboo*, was the work of a white woman, Nan Bagby Stevens; it was produced at the Greenwich Village Theatre with a white cast, but failed. In the early part of 1924 it was produced with an all-Negro cast, Charles Gilpin and Rose McClendon in the principal roles. Later Robeson replaced Gilpin in the role of the preacher. With these plays may be grouped *Goat Alley*, a play of Negro life in the back alleys of Washington, written by Ernest H. Culbertson, a white playwright, and produced with a Negro cast at the Bijou Theatre (New York), June 20, 1921. The play was well written and capably acted, but failed. In 1927 it was revived at the Princess Theatre without greater success.

But on May 15, 1924 Eugene O'Neill produced at the Provincetown Playhouse a Negro play that made New York and the rest of the country sit up and take notice. The play was *All God's Chillun Got Wings*. The cast was a mixed one, with Paul Robeson in the principal role, playing opposite Mary Blair, a white actress. Public excitement about this play did not wait for the opening in the theatre, but started fully three months before; that is, as soon as it was seen through the publication of the play in the *American Mercury* that the two chief characters were a coloured boy and a white girl, and that the boy falls in love with the girl and marries her. When it was learned that the play was to be produced in a New York theatre with a coloured and a white performer in these two roles, a controversy began in the newspapers of the city that quickly spread; and articles, editorials, and interviews filled columns upon columns in periodicals throughout the country. The discussion in the press was, as might be expected, more bitter than it had been in the incident of the Drama League dinner to Charles Gilpin. The New York *American* and the *Morning Telegraph* went further than other New York publications. For weeks they carried glaring headlines and inciting articles. They appeared to be seeking to provoke violence in order to stop the play.

The New York *American* on March 18, eight weeks before the opening, carried an article headed: "Riots Feared From Drama—'All God's Chillun' Direct Bid for Disorders, the View of George G. Battle— Thinks City Should Act." In the article George Gordon Battle was quoted as saying: "The production of such a play will be most unfortunate. If the Provincetown Players and Mr. O'Neill refuse to bow before public opinion, the city officials should take action to ban it from the stage." In the same article Mrs. W. J. Arnold, "a founder of the Daughters of the Confederacy," was quoted as saying: "The scene where Miss Blair is called upon to kiss and fondle a Negro's hand is going too far, even for the stage. The play may be produced above the Mason and Dixie [sic] line, but Mr. O'Neill will not get the friendly reception he had when he sent 'Emperor Jones' his other coloured play into the South. The play should be banned by the authorities, because it will be impossible for it to do otherwise than stir up ill feeling between the races."

An issue of the Hearst publication said editorially:

> Gentlemen who are engaged in producing plays should not make it any harder for their friends to protect them from censorship. They should not put on plays which are, or threaten to become, enemies of the public peace; they should not dramatize dynamite, because, while helping the box office, it may blow up the business.
>
> We refer to the play in which a white woman marries a black man and at the end of the play, after going crazy, stoops and kisses the Negro's hand.
>
> It is hard to imagine a more nauseating and inflammable situation, and in many communities the failure of the audience to scrap the play and mutilate the players would be regarded as a token of public anemia.

It would be still harder to imagine yellower journalism than this, or why a thing that has happened more than once in actual life should be regarded as so utterly beyond conception as a theatrical situation.

The opening night came, the theatre was crowded—the attacks had served as publicity—there was some feeling of tenseness on the part of the audience and a great deal on the part of the performers, but the play proceeded without any sign of antagonistic demonstration, without even a hiss or a boo. None of the appeals to prejudice, hate, and fear had had the intended effect. The pressure brought on Mayor Hylan and the Police Department got no further result than the refusal of permission to allow a group of children to appear in the opening scene. The public at large failed to be moved to any sense of impending danger to either the white or the black race because of this play. The outcome of the whole business proved that the rabid newspapers were not expressing public sentiment, but were striving to stir up a public sentiment.

All God's Chillun Got Wings did not prove to be another *Emperor Jones.* One sound reason why it did not was because it was not so good a play. It was dramatic enough, but the incidents did not link up along the inevitable line that the spectator was made to feel he must follow. It may be that as the play began to grow, Mr. O'Neill became afraid of it. At any rate, he side-stepped the logical question and let his heroine go crazy; thus shifting the question from that of a coloured man living with a white wife to that of a man living with a crazy woman; from which shift, so far as this particular play was concerned, nothing at all could be demonstrated. The play, as a play, did not please white people, and, on the other hand, it failed to please coloured people. Mr. O'Neill, perhaps in concession to public sentiment, made the white girl who is willing to marry the black student, and whom he is glad to get, about as lost as he could well make her. Coloured people not only did not consider this as any compliment to the race, but regarded it as absolutely contrary to the essential truth. However, the play ran for several weeks, and Paul Robeson increased his reputation by the restraint, sincerity, and dignity with which he acted a difficult role.

Mr. Robeson's reputation is now international. He played the leading Negro character in the London production of *Show Boat.* He played the title role in a successful revival of *The Emperor Jones* in Berlin early in 1930. And it has been announced that he will play Othello in a production to be made of Shakspere's immortal tragedy at the Savoy Theatre, London, in May 1930.

Perhaps it was now time for New York again to sing and dance and laugh with the Negro on the stage; and it soon had the opportunity. On October 29, 1924, exactly one year after the opening of *Runnin' Wild*, Florence Mills came to the Broadhurst Theatre in *Dixie to Broadway*, and New York had its first Negro revue. For the Florence Mills show broke away entirely from the established traditions of Negro musical comedy. Indeed, it had to, because she was the star; and the traditions called for a show built around two male comedians, usually of the black-face type. The revue was actually an enlarged edition of the one in which Miss Mills had been appearing at the Plantation. It was also the same revue that had been played in London the season before under the title of *Dover to Dixie* with her as the star. On the night of the production of *Dixie to Broadway* New York not only found itself with a novelty in the form of a Negro revue, but also discovered that it had a new artist of positive genius in the person of Florence Mills. She had made a name in *Shuffle Along*, but in *Dixie to Broadway* she was recognized for her full worth.

Florence Mills was born in Washington, D. C., January 25, 1895, and was on the stage practically all her life. She was a child prodigy and began her career before she was six years old as "Baby Florence Mills." As "Baby Florence" she appeared a number of times as a singing and dancing entertainer in the drawing-rooms of the diplomatic set at the capital. On one occasion Lady Pauncefote, wife of the British Ambassador, presented her with a gold bracelet. A very early photograph of Florence shows her in a pose calculated chiefly to display this piece of jewellery. The same photograph shows her wearing two medals, won through her skill in cake-walking and buck-dancing. She acquired these decorations as an amateur. Her first professional appearance on the stage was noted as follows in the Washington *Star*:

"The peerless child artist who has appeared before the most exclusive set in Washington, delighting them with her songs and dances, is appearing this week at the Empire Theater with the 'Sons of Ham' company No. 2. As an extra attraction is Baby Florence Mills singing 'Hannah from Savannah.' Baby Florence made a big hit and was encored for dancing."

After this debut she travelled for a while with a company as one of the "picks." Then she played in vaudeville with her two sisters, Olivia and Maude, in an act known as the Mills Sisters. Until she was twenty-five years old, she played from coast to coast in vaudeville or in one small road company or another, struggling hard, through that particularly hard sort of life, from a start of nine dollars a week up to four or five times that amount, and gaining a sure grasp on her art. Then, in the summer of 1921, in *Shuffle Along*, she came to Broadway—came from a Harlem cabaret to take the place of Gertrude Saunders—and fame and fortune met her there. Many of the good things of life came following; perhaps the best for her, after so many itinerant years, was the house she bought in Harlem, which her mother made home for her.

She left *Shuffle Along* to become the star of Lew Leslie's *Plantation Revue*. This revue proved so popular that Mr. Leslie took it to London. Miss Mills captured London completely. St. John Ervine, writing of her, said: "The success acquired by Miss Florence Mills, the American coloured girl playing in 'From *Dover to Dixie*' is something unequalled by any American playing here in the last decade. She is by far the most artistic person London has had the good fortune to see." When she returned from London, New York had the joy of seeing *Dixie to Broadway*.

In the spring of 1926 Miss Mills came out of the Plantation with a new revue called *Blackbirds*, and played at the Alhambra Theatre in Harlem for six weeks to packed houses. Early in the summer Mr. Leslie took the show to Paris, where it played for five months, then to London, where it had a six months' run. Miss Mills's popularity was unbounded. Her photographs were displayed everywhere, and her portrait was painted. News dispatches reported that the Prince of Wales was sixteen times a spectator of the revue, and that he always enthusiastically applauded "Little Twinks," and pronounced her "ripping."

"Ripping" will do, perhaps, as well as any other omnibus adjective in an attempt to define Florence Mills, but she was indefinable. One might best string out a list of words such as: pixy, elf, radiant, exotic, Peter Pan, wood-nymph, wistful, piquant, magnetism, witchery, madness, flame; and then despairingly exclaim: "Oh, you know what I mean." She could be whimsical, she could be almost grotesque; but she had the good taste that never allowed her to be coarse. She could be *risquée*, she could be seductive; but it was impossible for her to be vulgar, for she possessed a naivete that was alchemic. As a pantomimist and a singing and dancing comedienne she had no superior in any place or any race. And yet, after all, did she really sing? The upper range of her voice was full of bubbling, bell-like, bird-like tones. And there, perhaps, is the comprehensive word the Prince might have used: "bird-like." It was a rather magical thing Florence Mills used to do with that small voice in her favourite song, "I'm a Little Blackbird Looking for a Bluebird and she did it with such exquisite poignancy as always to raise a lump in your throat.

She got back to New York from the European tour of *Blackbirds* on October 12, 1927. She came back decided to have a delayed operation for appendicitis performed. She came back also with all the plans laid to follow the course taken with her former success, and present *Blackbirds* to Broadway. But *Blackbirds of 1928* was produced without her.

She died in the hospital, November 1, 1927. It it not an exaggeration to say that her death shocked the theatrical world. Harlem was stunned and at first refused to believe the news could be true. Then there followed vague rumours of foul play. The papers devoted columns to her, news and editorial. The *Evening Journal* and the *Evening Graphic* carried the story of her life in serial form. The Negroes of New York mourned her deeply, for she was more their idol than any other artist of the race. Her funeral was one such as Harlem, perhaps all New York, had never seen before. Five thousand people were packed to suffocation in Mother Zion Church. The air quivered with emotion. Hall Johnson's choir sang Spirituals, and the whole throng wept and sobbed. A fellow actress rose at the end of the service to sing a song dedicated to the dead star; she started, she faltered, she struggled on; her efforts ended in a frantic cry: "Florence!" and she swayed and collapsed in a heap on the floor. Women fainted and men were unnerved. Under all there could be sensed a bewilderment, a resentment, at this act of God—Why did He do it?—we have so few—she was so young—she might have done so much more for us in the eyes of the world.

Outside the church more than a hundred thousand people jammed the streets. A detail of one hundred and fifty police was necessary to handle the crowd. The procession moved slowly through this dense mass. Eleven automobiles conveyed the flowers. Thirty coloured girls from the stage, dressed alike in grey, walked as an escort. The cortege followed. As One Hundred and Forty-fifth Street was neared, an airplane circled low and released a flock of blackbirds. They fluttered overhead a few seconds and then flew away.

SEVENTEEN

I N OCTOBER 1925 THERE WAS PRODUCED at the Frolic Theatre (New York) a play that was a departure for the Negro in the theatre. It was a serious drama, written by a coloured playwright, played by a mixed cast of fourteen white and three coloured performers, and with a Negro as the principal character. The play was *Appearances*, and it was distinctively a play with a message; but, surprising as it may be, the message had nothing to do with race. The play was an exposition of the *Servant in the House* idea. It was, in fact, a sort of dramatization of the doctrines of Christian Science, of the doctrine that simply by willing our subconscious forces into action we can accomplish the seemingly impossible. The load of such a message is generally more than any play can carry; and *Appearances* was pretty heavily weighted. It was only because the preachments of cheerful uplift were rendered with such direct, almost childlike simplicity that a New York audience listened without impatience. But the second act of the play, a court scene in which the hero through a conspiracy is *almost* convicted of assaulting a white woman, did have dramatic power and was well acted. It was this act that carried the play along. *Appearances* received fairly good notices and drew audiences for several weeks, but it did not appeal strongly enough to the general public to last.

The story of the writer of the play was actually better drama than the play. He was Garland Anderson, the bellboy and switchboard operator in an apartment hotel in San Francisco. As such he came into intimate contact with the guests and did not hesitate to give them his cheerful philosophy of life. They thought it "beautiful" and "wonderful" and felt that he ought to reach more people with his message. For several years he pondered over how to do this. Then he saw a performance of Channing Pollock's *The Fool* and resolved to write a play. He wrote the play and showed it to a number of people in San Francisco, among them Richard Bennett, who gave him encouragement. Al Jolson heard of the play and wired the author to send him the manuscript. He did so and a few days later followed in person. When Mr. Anderson arrived in New York Mr. Jolson told him he was sorry he could not produce the play; he did, however, give him a splendid letter and paid the expenses of his trip from San Francisco and furnished him enough money for a stay of a couple of months in New York.

Mr. Anderson now set about to get a producer, but without success. Then he decided to give a public reading of the play. Despite discouragements, he secured the grand ball room of the Waldorf-Astoria Hotel and on a Sunday afternoon read the play to some six hundred people. He made a trip to Washington and presented a copy of the manuscript to President Coolidge. He returned to New York and gave another public reading at the Manhattan Opera House. On June 19, 1925 L. W. Sagar, manager of the Central Theatre, accepted the manuscript for production and gave Mr. Anderson an option to buy a half-interest in the play, good until September 15. With his contract in his pocket he returned immediately to San Francisco. His efforts in New York had consumed seven months. During that time he had secured the approval and help of David Belasco, Heywood Broun, Marjorie Rambeau, Nance O'Neill, Bill Robinson, and some others.

On his return to San Francisco he quickly sold a half-interest in the play to Messrs. H. S. and Fergus Wilkinson, guests at the hotel where he had worked, for fifteen thousand dollars. In two automobiles Mr. Anderson and his backers motored across the continent, the cars carrying streamers: *San Francisco to New York—For the Opening Production of Appearances—By Garland Anderson, the San Francisco Bellhop Playwright.* Before leaving San Francisco the party was photographed with Mr. Anderson receiving a letter from the Mayor of San Francisco to be delivered to the Mayor of New York. On arrival in New York the party was photographed in front of City Hall with Mr. Anderson delivering his letter to Mayor Hylan.

The run of the play was not long, but, through the efforts of Mr. Anderson, it gained a second production in New York. At the present time, through his still further efforts, it is being played in London at the Royalty Theatre and appears to be making a good impression. The play may not be an altogether convincing argument for the theories it advances, but the author himself is.

In February 1926 David Belasco produced at the Belasco Theatre the sensational melodrama *Lulu Belle*, with a cast of sixty or more persons, above three-fourths of whom were coloured. The title-role was played with great realism by Lenore Ulric, and Ruby Lee, a female role second in importance only to Miss Ulric's, was played by Evelyn Preer. Edna Thomas, who had played in the Ethiopian Art Company with Miss Preer, had a small part; later she replaced Miss Preer. The role of George Randall, the principal Negro male character, was finely played by Henry Hull, a white actor, whose make-up and dialect were beyond detection. The play was written by Edward Sheldon and Charles

MacArthur. The scenes of the four acts were: I, A street scene in the San Juan Hill district; II, the top floor of a Harlem boardinghouse; III, a Harlem cabaret; IV, five years later—a luxurious apartment in Paris. The story was that of the rise of a beautiful little coloured wanton from the sidewalks of Harlem to an apartment on the avenue Marigny, Paris, provided for her by the Vicomte de Villars. The story ended in tragedy. Because of the manner in which it set on the stage scenes from New York life that were wholly Negro, and because of the large number of coloured performers in a mixed cast playing important roles, *Lulu Belle* was extremely significant in the history of the Negro in the theatre in New York.

Later in the same season Paul Robeson appeared as the star in *Black Boy*, a play by Jim Tully and Frank Dazey, which dealt with the rise and fall of a Negro prize-fighter. It was produced at the Comedy Theatre. *Black Boy* was not a success and did not add much to Mr. Robeson's prestige. The cast was a mixed one. Freddie Washington, a coloured actress, gave a remarkable performance in the role of a coloured girl who, in the play, passes for white, but finally declares she is coloured and goes to live with *Black Boy*.

In October another play was produced in New York with a large mixed cast, in which Negro principals were integral parts. It was *Deep River*, an opera with book by Laurence Stallings and music by Frank Harling. It was produced by Arthur Hopkins at the Imperial Theatre. The scene of the opera was Creole New Orleans of 1835. The piece was beautifully mounted and well sung, but it did not remain long. Nevertheless, it was a step for the Negro. Three of the important parts were played by coloured performers. Charlotte Murray, a contralto, sang a principal role, as did Jules Bledsoe, then a student and now well known. This was Mr. Bledsoe's first appearance on the theatrical stage, and his singing in the voodoo scene was one of the highest spots of the opera.

In one of the scenes—the quadroon ball—there was a beautiful winding staircase, down which Rose McClendon had to come slowly—ever so slowly—and walk through a *patio*, then off stage. It was a high test for poise, grace, and aristocratic bearing. She accomplished this feat every night in a manner that won great applause. Quoting Alexander Woolcott in the New York *World*: "When 'Deep River' was having its trial flight in Philadelphia Ethel Barrymore slipped in to snatch what moments she could of it. 'Stay till the last act if you can,' Arthur Hopkins whispered to her, 'and watch Rose McClendon come down those stairs. She can teach some of our most hoity-toity actresses distinction.' It was Miss Barrymore who hunted *him* up after the performance to say, 'She can teach them *all* distinction.'"

Several white Southern playwrights had essayed a portrayal of some phase of Negro life in the South, but the first to succeed in the New York theatre was Paul Green, of the University of North Carolina. He had written a number of one-act plays of Southern Negro life, some of which had been produced by amateurs. On December 28, 1926 his *In Abraham's Bosom* was produced at the Provincetown Playhouse. *In Abraham's Bosom* was a beautiful though terrible play. It was closer and truer to actual Negro life and probed deeper into it than any drama of the kind that had yet been produced. There were twelve characters in the cast, ten coloured and two white. The Negro actors playing important parts were Rose McClendon, Abbie Mitchell, Frank Wilson, and Jules Bledsoe in the leading character. Later Frank Wilson replaced Mr. Bledsoe. Mrs. McClendon had acted and Mr. Bledsoe had sung two months before in *Deep River*. Before going on the stage, Mr. Bledsoe had been a student in medicine at Columbia University; and he had also for a long time been a student of music, especially of singing. He was divided within himself as to which line to follow, medicine or art. Whenever he was good enough to sing or play the piano or dance the Charleston (he is an expert), friends and acquaintances were unanimous in declaring that he ought to go on the stage. That, perhaps, may have helped him to decide. Like Robeson, who has made a national reputation as an athlete, as an actor, and as a singer, Bledsoe is a very versatile man. In *Deep River* he sang a heroic baritone role; in *In Abraham's Bosom* he played a dramatic and tragic part; and he was yet to play an entirely different character from either in *Show Boat*.

In Abraham's Bosom was a decided success. It enjoyed a long run and had several revivals. In 1927 it was awarded the Pulitzer Prize for the original American play best representing the educational value and power of the stage.

The New Playwrights produced *Earth*, by Em Jo Basshe, at the Fifty-second Street Theatre, March 9, 1927. *Earth* was a Negro play of considerable power, with religion and superstition as the main themes. The acting was creditable and there was also some effective singing. The entire cast was composed of coloured performers. The two leading roles were played by Inez Clough and Daniel Haynes. Miss Clough had long been known for her finished work; Mr. Haynes was a newcomer, but he made a splendid impression and demonstrated the potentialities he possessed.

In the summer of 1927, on June 11 and 12, two Negro musical plays were produced in New York: *Africana*, a revue, at the Sixty-third Street Theatre, with Ethel Waters as the star; and *Rang Tang*, a new Miller and Lyles musical comedy, at the Majestic Theatre. In *Rang Tang* Miller and Lyles were as funny as ever in a very good show. They had a droll scene in an airplane which had come down at sea before they had finished the flight they were making to Africa. The company was good.

Among the members were Evelyn Preer, Zaidie Jackson, and Daniel Haynes in a picturesque role as King of Madagascar, a part that gave his voice and physique great opportunities. But *Rang Tang* did not draw so well as its two predecessors. As one watched it, the thought arose that perhaps the traditional pattern of Negro musical comedy was a bit worn.

Africana opened the night before *Rang Tang*. It was a swift modern revue. There were several quite clever people in it, but Ethel Waters dominated the show. She did this nearly to the same degree that Florence Mills dominated her show, but with a technique almost in contrast. Miss Waters is tall, almost statuesque, with a head so beautiful that Antonio Salemmi asked the privilege of doing it in bronze—the piece was purchased by Carl Van Vechten. She is not so versatile as was Florence Mills; she has not the vivacious energy or the elusive charm; nor can she dance like the sprite Miss Mills was. Miss Waters gets her audiences, and she does get them completely, through an innate poise that she possesses; through the quiet and subtlety of her personality. She never "works hard" on the stage. Her bodily movements, when she makes them, are almost languorous. Indeed, she is at her best when she is standing perfectly still, singing quietly. Her singing corresponds to her bodily movements; she never over-exerts her voice; she always creates a sense of reserved power that compels the listener. Her singing has made a great many songs widely popular. "Dinah," and "I'm Coming, Virginia," are a part of her personality and fame. Miss Waters also has a disarming quality which enables her to sing some songs that many singers would not be able to get away with on the stage. Those who have heard her sing "Shake That Thing" will understand. Miss Waters began her career in a Harlem cabaret. She was engaged to take the lead in the Plantation revue in the absence of Florence Mills; at the same time Josephine Baker was in the chorus there. When Mrs. Reagan, a producer, was looking for a star to head the revue she was planning to put on in Paris, she went on a scouting trip to the Plantation. She tried to get Ethel Waters and, failing, took Josephine Baker; but that is really another story.

The reader has by now come to see that in this period of the Negro in the theatre the pendulum has swung or been made to swing from drama to music and from music to drama in something like regular intervals; and the pendulum now swung over to drama. On October 10 of this same year the Theatre Guild produced at the Guild Theatre *Porgy* by Dorothy and Du Bose Heyward. The play was a dramatization of Mr. Heyward's novel *Porgy*, one of the notable books of the year. Here was the second white Southerner—if in literary collaboration man and wife can be counted as one—to take Negro life in the South and work it into a successful play. *Porgy* was a folk-play and portrayed life among the Negroes of Catfish Row in Charleston, South Carolina—simple fisher-folk. The play carried conviction through its sincere simplicity. But it did not run along on a monotonous level; at times it rose to heights of ecstasy and tragedy; and always it was suffused with Negro humour. Not only was the play well written, but it was remarkably mounted and staged. In the closing scene of the first act—in which the company is gathered in Serena's room holding the wake over her murdered husband; singing and singing until they rise and break into religious frenzy, their swaying bodies and uplifted hands suddenly thrown in black shadows against the background of the whitewashed walls of the room; singing and singing—there have been few scenes in the New York theatre to equal it in emotional power. *Porgy* loomed high above every Negro drama that had ever been produced.

Equal to the writing and staging was the acting. The cast was a large one, sixty-six in all, with twenty-four principals, five of them white. Among the Negro principals the work of Frank Wilson as Porgy; Georgette Harvey as Maria, keeper of the cook-shop; Wesley Hill as Jake, captain of the fishing-fleet; Rose McClendon as Serena; and Evelyn Ellis as Crown's Bess, was outstanding. And far above medium was the work of Jack Carter as Crown, Leigh Whipper in the two roles of the undertaker and the crab-man, A. B. Comathiere as Simon Frazier, a lawyer, and Percy Verwayne as Sporting Life. In *Porgy* the Negro performer removed all doubts as to his ability to do acting that requires thoughtful interpretation and intelligent skill. Here was more than the achievement of one or two individuals who might be set down as exceptions. Here was a large company giving a first-rate, even performance, with eight or ten reaching a high mark. The evidence was massive and indisputable. *Porgy* was one of the great theatrical successes of the decade. It ran altogether in New York, in London, and on the road for more than two years.

Back swung the pendulum to music, singing, and dancing; and early in 1928 Lew Leslie produced *Blackbirds of 1928* at the Liberty Theatre (New York). *Blackbirds* set a pace for all revues, white as well as black. The show became a sort of New York institution; and out-of-town visitors came to the city with the conviction that it was something that had to be seen. Like *Shuffle Along*, it started several songs on a trip round the world. Those songs were: "I Can't Give You Anything but Love," "Magnolia's Wedding Day," "Diga Diga Do," and "I Must Have That Man." But above and beyond the singing of these songs was the singing in the burlesque of the wake scene from *Porgy*. This burlesque scene was staged similarly to the original, even to the shadows on the wall. But instead of Spirituals the blues—the "St. Louis Blues"—were sung, and with an effect equally electrical and almost as moving. This effect must have suggested even to the unthinking the close analogy, which does exist, between the Negro folk-songs known as Spirituals and those known as blues. William Bolitho, writing about *Blackbirds* in the *World*, said of this scene:

> They sang for the dead, in a shadowy chapel, in long prison-coloured overalls, shaking themselves, the shadows behind them, then the whole auditorium, and then at last I even thought of that most stable, buried thing in the whole universe, the biodynamic instincts of the human personality, with their great ancestral rhythms.

The great success of *Blackbirds* was mainly an ensemble success, a success of the whole company and the very excellent band. For while there were in the cast two very clever girls, Adelaide Hall and Ada Ward, and a fairly funny comedian, there was only one individual performer who stood out pre-eminently, and that was Bill Robinson. The same Bill Robinson had been a vaudeville head-liner for a good many years, but he was new to audiences in the legitimate theatres and utterly unknown to most of the dramatic critics. He was immediately pronounced the greatest tap-dancer in the world, and in a few weeks he was one of the most widely known men in the city. His stunt of dancing up and down a set of stair steps—a stunt that has since been much imitated—was acknowledged as a demonstration of the utmost perfection in tapping out intricate rhythms. The nicety with which each group of rhythms was executed was marvellous and never failed to give the listening spectator pleasurable surprise at the accomplishment of the feat.

A great deal was written about the dancing of Bill Robinson; probably as much as was ever written about any visiting Spanish or

Russian dancer. Much of what was written was a serious consideration of his art. Mary Austin, writing in the *Nation* and making an analysis of the aesthetics underlying Mr. Robinson's work, said in part:

". . . He is proud of being able with the tappings of his feet to produce and coordinate more distinct simultaneous rhythms than any other American dancer. And by the postures of his lithe dark body and the motions of his slender cane so punctuate this rhythmic patter as to restore, for his audience, the primal freshness of their own lost rhythmic powers. It is only by the sincere unconsciousness of his genius that he is able to attain that perfection of stage performance, in which his audience is made happily to participate. For Bill Robinson does not know intellectually that the capacity for rhythmic coordination is the fundament, not only of art but all human achievement.

"Robinson is intelligent about his audience to the extent of having his own pleasure and competence in his dancing enhanced by this, and by that delicate concealment of effort—the noblesse of the aristocracy of art—by which the audience is left intact in its privilege of enjoyment. Those swift-vanishings from the stage to wipe away the sweat of muscles constrained to their uttermost, and bright-returns, having all the intriguing quality of bird flight, are as carefully studied as the lifting and placing of the cane are faithfully rehearsed. But they are all done after the fashion of true genius, which senses its effects rather than rationalizes them.

". . . One has to be slightly tone deaf or a superior mathematician to realize how much the appreciation of spatial relations has to do with our enjoyment of musical harmony. It is safe to say that Bill Robinson's audience knows no more than Bill of what, without any diminution of frank pleasure, is going on before its eyes. It probably does not realize in any formal way that he is offering them the great desideratum of modern art, a clean short cut to areas of enjoyment long closed to us by the accumulated rubbish of the culture route. For Bill Robinson not only restores to us our primal rhythmic appreciations; he himself reaches the sources of his rhythmic inspiration by paths that the modem American artist would give one of his eyes—the eye Aimed and colored by Ave thousand years of absorbed culture—to feel beneath his feet. . . .

"One suspects, too, a dawning appreciation on the part of such (American) audiences that in such release and return lies the chief gift of the Negro to contemporary art. . . ."

Blackbirds of 1928 ran at the one theatre in New York for more than a year; a second company toured other cities of the country.

A little before the opening of *Blackbirds* a unique venture was made at the Princess Theatre (New York). It was the presentation of a serious play written and produced as well as acted by Negroes. The play was *Meek Mose*, written by Frank Wilson and produced by Lester A. Walton. In the cast were a number of well-known and capable performers. Charles H. Moore played the principal role; among those supporting him were Sidney Kirkpatrick, Laura Bowman, and Susie Sutton. In addition to playing on the stage, Mr. Wilson had written several sketches and plays that had been produced in Harlem. It was the writing of plays while he was still a post-office employee that led him to the stage. But *Meek Mose* failed to interest Broadway.

Three weeks later, on February 27, Miller and Lyles appeared again on Broadway; this time at the theatre of their first good fortune, the Sixty-third Street. The show was called *Keep Shufflin'*, and, while far from being another *Shuffle Along*, it was also far from being a poor show. One thing, however, it seemed to demonstrate pretty clearly— that the traditional Negro musical-comedy pattern was about worn out or, at least, needed to be left unused for a time. In the meanwhile two great musical plays with mixed casts were playing in New York, *Golden Dawn* at Hammerstein's Theatre and *Show Boat* at the Ziegfeld Theatre. In each of these companies there were some forty to fifty coloured performers. In *Show Boat* Jules Bledsoe played one of the featured parts, a character that ran straight through the play, and sang the most popular number of the whole show, "Old Man River."

On February 2, 1929 a play was put on at the Apollo Theatre that was in more ways than one sensational. It was a melodramatic play of Negro life in New York. It was far removed from *In Abraham's Bosom* and *Porgy*. It had no touch even with *All God's Chillun Got Wings*. The play was called *Harlem* and it was a portrayal of life in a Harlem railroad flat, of rent parties, of the "sweetback," of the "hot stuff man," of the "number king" and the number racket. And it also portrayed a distracted migrant mother from the South caught in this whirlpool and struggling to save herself, her husband, and her children from being submerged. The play depicted a low level of life, but it had vitality and power. The cast was large, sixty in number, all Negroes, except one. The acting was extremely realistic. The work of Inez Clough as the mother; Isabell Washington, a sister of Freddie Washington, as the wayward daughter; Ernest Whitman as the number king; and Billy Andrews as one of his runners, was especially good. Furthermore, the play was the work of a Negro writer, Wallace Thurman, in collaboration with William Jourdan, a white writer. It was a success.

In the summer of 1929 *Hot Chocolates*, the revue from Connie's Inn, a Harlem night-club, opened downtown at the Hudson Theatre. The piece was very fast, and it was funny and tuneful. The company disclosed no Florence Mills or Ethel Waters or Bill Robinson, but it did contain some very clever performers. A diminutive bit of femininity called Baby Cox made a hit. Her dancing was as fast as anything New York had ever seen. Nor did *Hot Chocolates* contain a list of song hits like *Shuffle Along* and *Blackbirds*, but one of its songs, "Ain't Misbehavin'," did have quite a vogue. It ran in New York about six months and on the road several months longer.

In *Porgy* the Negro removed any lingering doubts as to his ability to do intelligent acting. In *The Green Pastures* he established conclusively his capacity to get the utmost subtleties across the footlights, to convey the most delicate nuances of emotion, to create the atmosphere in which the seemingly unreal becomes for the audience the most real thing in life. *The Green Pastures* is a play so simple and yet so profound, so close to the earth and yet so spiritual, that it is as high a test for those powers in the actor as any play the American stage has seen—a higher test than many of the immortalized classics. It is a play in which the line between the sublime and the ridiculous is so tenuous that the slightest strain upon it would bring the whole play tumbling down. Take the place that Heywood Broun pointed out where the coloured angels are holding a fish fry in heaven, and the audience is chuckling over the little black cherub with a bone in his throat, and suddenly through the laughter rings out Gabriel's great line: "Gangway for the Lord God Jehovah!"

As Mr. Broun says, it is the most stupendous entrance ever arranged for any actor. And if the audience should laugh when the actor appears, the play would be about done for. And no one laughs. The acting in *The Green Pastures* seems so spontaneous and natural that one is tempted to believe the players are not really acting. In the light of the truth about the matter, this is a high compliment.

The Green Pastures was produced at the Mansfield Theatre on February 26, 1930. It is the work of Marc Connelly and was suggested by Roark Bradford's Southern sketches *Ol' Man Adam and His Chillun*. Mr. Connelly describes it as "an attempt to present certain aspects of a living religion in the terms of its believers. The religion is that of thousands of Negroes in the deep South." What Mr. Connelly actually did was to work something very little short of a miracle. No one seems able to remember any playwright, play, and company of players that have together received such unanimous praise as these three factors in the making of *The Green Pastures*. Almost as valuable as either of these factors is the work of the Hall Johnson Choir in singing the Spirituals. It serves to blend all the efforts into a magical whole. And there is something akin to poetic justice in the fact that Robert Edmond Jones, who by his work in 1917 with the Hapgood Coloured Players gave an earnest of his faith in the future, should have the satisfaction of bringing his larger experience and surer technique to *The Green Pastures*. The play was awarded the Pulitzer prize for 1929. In making their recommendation the jurors stated:

> One play—*The Green Pastures* by Marc Connelly—towers so far above the other American plays of the season and comes so near to setting a new standard of excellence for the American drama of all time that the jurors desire with

unusual enthusiasm to recommend it for the Pulitzer prize.
. . . On this occasion, the jurors state emphatically that they
have no second choice.

The cast is a large one and entirely coloured. It is headed by
Richard B. Harrison, who plays God; and it is probable that no role
more difficult or delicate was ever essayed on the stage; yet it does
not seem possible that it could be more perfectly played. This is Mr.
Harrison's first appearance on the professional stage, but for more than
thirty years he has been a dramatic reader, giving readings for the most
part in coloured churches and before coloured schools. For a long time
he has carried an ambition to play a part that "fitted his personality," and
a firm conviction that he would make good if he ever got the chance.
The chance did not come until he was past sixty—but what a chance!

At least twenty parts in which the acting is of high merit could be
singled out; but mention of the play cannot be made without mention
also of the work of Wesley Hill, of *Porgy* fame, in the role of the Angel
Gabriel, Daniel Haynes in the two roles of Adam and Hezdrel, Josephine
Byrd and Florence Fields as the two charwomen who clean the Lord's
private office, Tutt Whitney as Noah, and Charles H. Moore as Mr.
Deshee. The complete program of the play is found on the following
pages:

Laurence Rivers

The Green Pastures

A Fable by

Marc Connelly

Production Designed by Robert Edmond Jones
Music Under the Direction of Hall Johnson
Play Staged by the Author

Cast of Characters

(In the Order of Their Appearance)

Mr. Deshee	Charles H. Moore
Myrtle	Alicia Escamilla
First Boy	Jazzlips Richardson, Jr.
Second Boy	Howard Washington
Third Boy	Reginald Blythwood
Randolph	Joe Byrd
A Cook	Frances Smith
Custard Maker	Homer Tutt
First Mammy Angel	Anna Mae Fritz
A Stout Angel	Josephine Byrd
A Slender Angel	Edna Thrower
Archangel	J. A. Shipp
Gabriel	Wesley Hill
The Lord	Richard B. Harrison
Choir Leader	McKinley Reeves
Adam	Daniel L. Haynes
Eve	Inez Richardson Wilson
Cain	Lou Vernon
Cain's Girl	Dorothy Randolph
Zeba	Edna M. Harris
Cain the Sixth	James Fuller
Boy Gambler	Louis Kelsey

First Gambler	Collington Hayes
Second Gambler	Ivan Sharp
Voice in Shanty	Josephine Byrd
Noah	Tutt Whitney
Noah's Wife	Susie Sutton
Shem Milton	J. Williams
First Woman	Dinks Thomas
Second Woman	Anna Mae Fritz
Third Woman	Geneva Blythwood
First Man	Emory Richardson
Flatfoot	Freddie Archibald
Ham J.	Homer Tutt
Japheth	Stanleigh Morrell
First Cleaner	Josephine Byrd
Second Cleaner	Florence Fields
Abraham	J. A. Shipp
Isaac	Charles H. Moore
Jacob	Edgar Burks
Moses	Alonzo Fenderson
Zipporah	Mercedes Gilbert
Aaron	McKinley Reeves
A Candidate Magician	Reginald Fenderson
Pharaoh	George Randol
The General	Walt McClane
First Wizard	Emory Richardson
Head Magician	Arthur Porter
Joshua	Stanleigh Morrell
First Scout	Ivan Sharp
Master of Ceremonies	Billy Cumby
King of Babylon	Jay Mondaaye
Prophet	Ivan Sharp
High Priest	J. Homer Tutt

The King's Favorites	Leona Winkler
	Florence Lee
	Constance Van Dyke
	Mary Ella Hart
	Inez Persand

Officer	Emory Richardson
Hezdrel	Daniel L. Haynes
Another Officer	Stanleigh Morrell

The Children

Philistine Bumgardner, Margery Bumgardner, Fredia Longshaw, Wilbur Cohen, Jr., Verdon Perdue, Ruby Davis, Willmay Davis, Margerette Thrower, Viola Lewis.

Angels and Townspeople

Amy Escamilla, Elsie Byrd, Benveneta Washington, Thula Oritz, Ruth Carl, Geneva Blythwood.

Babylonian Band

Carl Shorter, Earl Bowie, Thomas Russell, Richard Henderson.

The Choir

Evelyn Burwell, Assistant Director

Sopranos—Bertha Wright, Geraldine Gooding, Marie Warren, Mattie Harris, Elsie Thompson, Massie Patterson, Marguerite Avery.

Altos—Ruthena Matson, Leona Avery, Mrs. Willie Mays, Viola Mickens, Charlotte Junius.

Tenors—John Warner, Joe Loomis, Walter Hilliard, Harold Foster, Adolph Henderson, William McFarland, McKinley Reeves, Arthur Porter.

Baritones—Marc D'Albert, Gerome Addison, Walter Whitfield, D. K. Williams.

Bassos—Lester Holland, Cecil McNair, Tom Lee, Walter Meadows, Frank Horace.

Synopsis of Scenes Part I: Scene 1—The Sunday School. Scene 2—A Fish Fry. Scene 3—A Garden. Scene 4—Outside the Garden. Scene 5—A Roadside. Scene 6—A Private Office. Scene 7—Another Roadside. Scene 8—A House. Scene 9—A Hillside. Scene 10—A Mountain Top.

Part II: Scene 1—The Private Office. Scene 2—The Mouth of a Cave. Scene 3—A Throne Room. Scene 4—The Foot of a Mountain. Scene 5—A Cabaret. Scene 6—The Private Office. Scene 7—Outside a Temple. Scene 8—Another Fish Fry.

The past seventy-five years have seen vast changes in the position of the Negro in the theatre. Beginning as a mere butt of laughter, he has worked on up through minstrelsy and the musical-comedy shows to become a creator of laughter; to become a maker of songs and dances for the people. This alone is an achievement not to be despised. The past twenty years have seen the Negro actor, after a set-back, emerge from the Negro theatre of Harlem and finally make for himself a definite place on the legitimate stage of New York, the theatrical capital of the world. The last ten years have seen the growth of a list, surprisingly long considering all the conditions, of names that are known in connexion with the theatre: Charles Gilpin, Paul Robeson, Jules Bledsoe, Frank Wilson, Daniel Haynes, Wesley Hill, Charles H. Moore, Richard B. Harrison, Florence Mills, Rose McClendon, Evelyn Ellis, Ethel Waters, Inez Clough, Abbie Mitchell, Evelyn Preer, F. E. Miller, Aubrey Lyles, Noble Sissle, Eubie Blake, Johnny Hudgins, and Bill Robinson. The list can be stretched to take in Josephine Baker, now of Europe and South America, and Turner Layton and Tandy Johnstone, now of London. Josephine Baker was not wholly unknown before her name became a household word in Europe; when she was with Sissle and Blake's *Chocolate Dandies* she was the real box-office attraction. She was only in the chorus, but was paid one hundred and twenty-five dollars a week and advertised as the highest paid chorus girl in the world. Billy Pierce, though he is not on the stage and though his influence has been exerted almost entirely through the white performer, cannot be omitted from this list. Mr. Pierce conducts a large and successful studio where he teaches dancers the art of tapping out intricate Negro rhythms with their feet. In the same category is Will Vodery, who for years has scored jazz orchestral arrangements for the Florenz Ziegfeld productions and for other Broadway musical shows. In this field Mr. Vodery stands among the foremost. He is at present on the staff of arrangers of the Fox Film Company.

As the progress of this period is traced, it can be seen that it is the Negro as an actor that has gained ground, gained in experience and in technique, and raised his position higher and higher in the world of the theatre. The Negro as a writer for the theatre has not kept pace; he has, in fact, lost ground, even in the special field where he was once prominent, the field of Negro musical shows. In the serious drama three attempts have been made in the professional theatre, only one of which was successful. Coloured people often complain about the sort of light that is shed upon the race in most Negro plays. It may be—there is no certainty—that their remedy lies in the development of Negro playwrights. Some good reasons can be assigned for this discrepancy between the status of the actor and of the playwright, but they do not alter the fact.

The relation of Harlem to the latest phase of the development of the Negro in the theatre cannot be overlooked. New York is the centre from which all the main forces and activities of the American theatre radiate. And Harlem, with its cosmopolitan Negro population, its literary and artistic groups, its theatres, its cabarets and night-clubs, its theatrical clubs, and its little-theatre movement, with all of its elements that fire ambition, its opportunities for the nurture and development of talent, is within the radius of that centre. Here, then, was the field, and here were those best fitted to occupy it. There is no other city in the country where the same thing could have happened; and it could not have happened in New York had there been no Harlem at hand.

There are three other lines along which the Negro in New York has moved forward; three lines leading to the phonograph, radio, and screen audiences. For a long while Negroes have been making phonograph records. There have been jubilee singers, singers of Spirituals and of Negro comic songs. Bert Williams's royalties from the sale of his records was a very considerable sum. Roland Hayes, Paul Robeson, J. Rosamond Johnson, Taylor Gordon, and other artists have made records. But probably the Negro artists most popular with the phonograph audiences are the great singers of blues. The three Smiths, Mamie, Bessie, and Clara—not sisters—are known by all listeners to blues through the phonograph. It was Carl Van Vechten who first pointed out that the blues-singers were artists. When Mr. Van Vechten, by his articles in *Vanity Fair* and other publications, and by his personal efforts, was doing so much to focus public attention upon the recent literary and artistic emergence of the Negro and upon the individual artists, he did not neglect the singers of this important and not fully evaluated genre of Negro folk-songs. In a *Vanity Fair* article (March 1926) he wrote of the singing of Ethel Waters, Bessie Smith, and Clara Smith and gave the following impression of Clara singing not from a record, but from a theatre stage:

> Clara is a crude purveyor of the pseudo-folk-songs of her race. She employs, however, more nuances of expression

than Bessie. Her voice flutters agonizingly between tones. Music critics would say that she sings off key. What she really does, of course, is to sing quarter tones. Thus she is justifiably billed as the "World's greatest moaner." She appears to be more of an artist than Bessie, but I suspect that this apparent artistry is spontaneous and uncalculated.

As she comes upon the stage through folds of electric blue hangings at the back, she is wrapped in a black evening cloak bordered with white fur. She does not advance, but hesitates, turning her face in profile. The pianist is playing the characteristic strain of the Blues. Clara begins to sing:

"All day long I'm worried;
All day long I'm blue;
I'm so awfully lonesome,
I doan know what to do;
So I ask yo\ doctor,
See if you can fin'
Somethin' in yo' satchel To pacify my min'.
(Her tones become poignantly pathetic; tears roll down her cheeks.)
Write me a prescription fo' duh Blues,
De mean ole Blues."
(Her voice dies away in a mournful wail of pain and she buries her head in the curtains.)

Clara Smith's tones uncannily take on the colour of the saxophone; again of the clarinet. Her voice is powerful or melancholy, by turn. It tears the blood from one's heart. One learns from her that the Negro's cry to a cruel Cupid is as moving and elemental as is his cry to God, as expressed in the Spirituals.

Indeed, the blues are as essentially folk-songs as the Spirituals. In the one the Negro expresses his religious reactions to hopes of a blissful life hereafter; in the other he expresses his secular and profane reaction to the ills of the present existence. In the Spirituals it is the exultant shout or the sorrow-laden cry of the group; in the blues it is always the plaint of the individual. It is my opinion that the blues are of more value as the repository of folk-poetry than of folk-music. Very often there is the flash of lines that have great primitive beauty and power.

Negroes broadcast from most of the important radio stations in New York. Some of these stations have coloured broadcasters regularly employed. From time to time groups are engaged by the manufacturing concerns that advertise over the radio, to furnish the entertainment on their programs. Indeed, Negro programs are now so popular that there are quite a number of white broadcasters who are doing Negro "stuff." The great favourites among these at present are Amos and Andy, whose imitations are so good that they are extremely popular with coloured people. Their work and style are very close to what Miller and Lyles first employed. Their vocabulary, especially the misuse of the letter "r " in such coined words as "regusted," is almost identical with the vocabulary made classic by the two Negro comedians. But radio offers less gain to the Negro in mere racial prestige than either the phonograph or the screen. The radio, though it seems so direct, is, after all, quite impersonal. One does not visualize the person, nor does one have any permanent record of his work.

As New York is the centre of the theatre, Los Angeles is the centre of the movies; nevertheless, New York furnishes a large proportion of the artists who appear on the screen. *Hallelujah* is the most recent of the more stupendous Negro screen productions, and King Yidor recruited and organized the company for it in New York and later transported the whole outfit to Los Angeles. His reason for doing so must have been that he considered New York the greatest source upon which he could draw for the best Negro talent.

The Negro as a race has not fared so well on the screen as on the stage. New York would probably go to the theatre to see any first-class performance by Negroes. But moving pictures are not made for one theatre or one city or even one section of the country; they are made to suit everybody as nearly as possible; so they are built on the greatest common denominator of public opinion and public sentiment. In no moving picture, then, has any Negro screen actor been permitted to portray as high a type as has been portrayed on the stage.

EIGHTEEN

A T THE BEGINNING OF THE YEAR 1917 Negro Harlem was well along the road of development and prosperity. There was plenty of work, with a choice of jobs, and there was plenty of money. The community was beginning to feel conscious of its growing size and strength. It had entirely rid itself of the sense of apology for its existence. It was beginning to take pride in itself as Harlem, a Negro community.

But it was far from being complacent. It was alive and quick with enthusiasm and energy. Plans were being drawn that took in many things which hitherto had been considered to lie in the field of the impossible. Even its members from the darkest South felt strange stirrings of aspiration and shed that lethargy born of hopelessness which so often marks Negroes from sections where they have for generation after generation borne physically and spiritually an unrelieved weight of white superiority. Harlem had begun to dream of greater and greater things.

There had also taken place a birth of new ideas—new, at least, to Negroes. There were Negroes in Harlem who envisaged the situation of the race' in the light of economic and social revolution. Radicalism in the modern and international sense of the term was bom. Nightly along Lenox and Seventh avenues dozens of speakers could be heard explaining to listening groups the principles of socialism and the more revolutionary doctrines; trying to show them how these principles applied to their condition; hammering away at their traditional attitude of caution. These were some of the important forces at work in Harlem when the United States declared war against the German Empire.

Like the average American community, Harlem did not exhibit any great enthusiasm about the war. However, the war for months had been a topic of discussion among high and low, educated and uneducated. As the probabilities that this country would be embroiled became greater, the discussions increased in frequency and intensity. Among those who had a knowledge of affairs outside of the United States, there had all along been deep sympathy for France, as the most liberal of all great white nations towards black peoples. Among others there had been little concern one way or the other. The matter did not touch their lives; and when they were brought face to face with it, they were apt to brush it aside with characteristic Negro humour. One coloured man came into a Harlem barber-shop where a spirited discussion of the war was going on. When asked if he wasn't going to join the Army and fight the Germans, he replied amidst roars of laughter: "The Germans ain't done nothin' to me, and if they have, I forgive 'em."

Nevertheless, after the declaration of war, patriotism was fanned to a flame as quickly in Harlem as in the average American community. Indeed, six years before the United States entered the World War, steps were taken, led by the Equity Congress, a civic organization, to form a regiment of state militia. A provisional regiment was formed with Charles W. Filmore as provisional colonel. But a great deal of unwillingness and opposition developed on the part of state authorities to the mustering of the regiment. Several bills to that end were introduced in the Assembly, and those behind the proposal worked without ceasing; but it was not until July 2, 1913 that legislation authorizing the Fifteenth Regiment as a unit of the New York National Guard was passed. Immediately after the declaration of war the Federal Government recognized the regiment as a National Guard unit; and four months later, it was called to arms. It was the first regiment of the New York Guard to reach the required war strength.

The Fifteenth Regiment, under the command of Colonel William Hayward, after being awhile at Peekskill and at Camp Whitman, was sent to Spartanburg, South Carolina, where other units of the New York Guard were encamped. One day Sergeant Noble Sissle (the same Sissle of later *Shuffle Along* fame) went into the lobby of the local hotel, where there was a news-stand, to buy New York papers for himself and some of the men. The proprietor demanded of him why he did not take off his hat. Sergeant Sissle, in ignorance or defiance of the local mores, replied that he was a United States soldier and did not have to take off his hat. His hat was knocked off and he was kicked into the street. When the news of this incident reached camp, the men of the Fifteenth were for going into town and retaliating; but they were restrained by discipline. Men of other regiments of the New York Guard were indignant over the matter. The upshot of it all was that the Fifteenth Regiment was quickly ordered away and brought up to Camp Mills, on Long Island, where they were quartered with state troops from Alabama and Mississippi. The first night in camp trouble broke out over the discrimination against Negro soldiers in the canteen. The next day the regiment was hurriedly embarked. It sailed for France on November 12, 1917, being one of the first units from the National Guard of the whole country to go overseas; and this was, of course, long before any drafted troops were sent.

When the Fifteenth reached France there was further embarrassment. What to do with this Negro regiment became a serious question. Naturally, it should have remained a contingent of the New York National Guard; but for reasons held sufficient by those in high command, this could not be permitted. A way out was found by brigading the regiment with French troops. It was attached as a combat regiment to the Eighth Corps of the Fourth French Army. So, wholly under French command and carrying its state colours, it fought through the war. It was the only American unit to do either of these things. But "the stone that the builders rejected . . ." The first soldier of the entire American Expeditionary Forces to receive the Croix de Guerre with star and palm was Sergeant Henry Johnson of the Fifteenth Regiment, New York National Guard. The entire regiment was cited for exceptional valour in action during the Meuse-Argonne offensive, and its colours were decorated with the Croix de Guerre. The Fifteenth was under shell-fire 191 days, and held one trench ninety-one days without relief. At the declaration of the armistice, the French command gave it the honour of being the first of all the Allied forces to set foot on enemy territory; it went down as the advance guard of the French army of occupation. On this side, no single regiment in the A.E.F. was more often heard of or better known than the Fifteenth.

The regiment, now the 369th Infantry, arrived back in New York on February 12, 1919. On February 17 they paraded up Fifth Avenue. New York had seen lots of soldiers marching off to the war, but this was its first sight of marching veterans. The beautiful Victory Arch erected by the city at Madison Square as a part of the welcome to the returning troops was just nearing completion, and the old Fifteenth was the first body of troops to pass under it. The parade had been given great publicity, and the city was anxious and curious to see soldiers back from the trenches. The newspapers had intimated that a good part of the celebration would be hearing the now famous Fifteenth band play jazz and seeing the Negro soldiers step to it. Those who looked for that sort of entertainment were disappointed. Lieutenant Jim Europe walked sedately ahead, and Bandmaster Eugene Mikell had the great band alternate between two noble French military marches. And on the part of the men, there was no prancing, no showing of teeth, no swank; they marched with a steady stride, and from under their battered tin hats eyes that had looked straight at death were kept to the front.

But before the Fifteenth left for France, while they were in camp, training to go, there was another parade. On July 28, 1917 ten thousand New York Negroes silently marched down Fifth Avenue to the sound of muffled drums. The procession was headed by little children dressed in white, followed by the women in white, the men bringing up the rear. They carried banners. Some of them read: "Unto the Least of My Brethren," "Mother, Do Lynchers Go to Heaven?" "Give Me a Chance to Live," "Mr. President, Why Not Make America Safe for Democracy?" "Treat Us so that We May Love Our Country," "Patriotism and Loyalty Presuppose Protection and Liberty," "Pray for the Lady Macbeths of East St. Louis." In front of the man bearing the flag of the United States went a banner with the inscription: "Your Hands Are Full of Blood." This was the "Silent Protest Parade," organized by Negro leaders in Harlem, and one of the strangest and most impressive sights New York has witnessed. They marched in silence and they were watched in silence; but some of those who watched turned away with their eyes filled. Negro boy scouts distributed to the watchers circulars which, under the caption: "Why We March," stated these reasons for the demonstration:

We march because by the Grace of God and the force of truth, the dangerous, hampering walls of prejudice and inhuman injustices must fall.

We march because we want to make impossible a repetition of Waco, Memphis, and East St. Louis, by rousing the conscience of the country and bringing the murderers of our brothers, sisters and innocent children to justice.

We march because we deem it a crime to be silent in the face of such barbaric acts.

We march because we are thoroughly opposed to Jim-Crow Cars, Segregation, Discrimination, Disfranchisement, LYNCHING and the host of evils that are forced on us. It is time that the Spirit of Christ should be manifested in the making and execution of laws.

We march because we want our children to live in a better land and enjoy fairer conditions than have fallen to our lot.

We march in memory of our butchered dead, the massacre of the honest toilers who were removing the reproach of laziness and thriftlessness hurled at the entire race. They died to prove our worthiness to live. We live in spite of death shadowing us and ours. We prosper in the face of the most unwarranted and illegal oppression.

In view of the temper of the times, the Protest Parade was a courageous form of action to take. Behind all lay a culminating series of causes: lynchings, disfranchisement in the South, discriminations of many kinds, all of which assumed a magnified and more ironic cruelty in the face of the fact that Negroes were being called upon like all others to do their full part in the war as American citizens. But more immediate were the humiliations and injustices to which Negroes who had answered the call to arms were being subjected. And the cup overflowed with the East St. Louis massacre of July 2, 1917, in which four hundred thousand dollars' worth of property was destroyed, nearly six thousand Negroes driven from their homes, and hundreds murdered, a number of them burned alive in houses set afire over their heads. A resolution was introduced in Congress calling for an investigation of the East St. Louis riots. Some idea of the unbelievable savagery and its reaction upon the coloured people of the country may be gained from statements made at a hearing before the Committee on Rules of the House of Representatives by members of Congress.

Mr. Dyer of Missouri said in part:

I have visited out there and have interviewed a number of people and talked with a number who saw the murders that were committed. One man in particular who spoke to me is now an officer in the United States Army Reserve Corps, Lieut. Arbuckle, who is here in Washington somewhere, he having come here to report to the Adjutant General.

At the time of these happenings he was in the employ of the Government, but he was there on some business in East St. Louis. He said that he saw a part of this killing, and he saw them burning railway cars in yards, which were waiting for transport, filled with interstate commerce. He saw members of the militia of Illinois shoot Negroes. He saw policemen of the city of East St. Louis shoot Negroes. He saw this mob go to the homes of these Negroes and nail boards up over the doors and windows and then set fire and burn them up. He saw them take little children out of the arms of their mothers and throw them into the fires and bum them up. He saw the most dastardly and most criminal outrages ever perpetrated in this country, and this is undisputed. And I have talked with others; and my opinion is that over five hundred people were killed on this occasion.

Mr. Rodenberg of Illinois (East St. Louis is in Illinois), among other things, said:

Now, the plain, unvarnished truth of the matter, as Mr. Joyce told Secretary Baker, is that civil government in East St. Louis completely collapsed at the time of the riot. The conditions there at the time beggar description. It is impossible for any human being to describe the ferocity and brutality of that mob. In one case, for instance, a little ten-year-old boy, whose mother had been shot down, was running around sobbing and looking for his mother, and some members of the mob shot the boy, and before life had passed from his body they picked the little fellow up and threw him in the flames.

Another colored woman with a little two-year-old baby in her arms was trying to protect the child, and they shot her and also shot the child, and threw them in the flames. The horror of that tragedy in East St. Louis can never be described. It weighted me down with a feeling of depdesion that I did not recover from for weeks. The most sickening things I ever heard of were described in the letters that I received from home giving details of that attack.

The Silent Protest Parade had hardly disbanded when there flashed up from Texas the news of the "Houston affair." A battalion of the Twenty-fourth Infantry, one of the Negro regiments of the regular Army, was stationed at the time at Houston, and during their service there a number of the men had been assaulted by the Houston police. The friction grew out of the fact that, instead of having the soldiers of the camp policed by the usual method of establishing a provost guard, that duty was placed in the hands of the local police. The most popular noncommissioned officer, and one of the most experienced soldiers in the regiment, Corporal Baltimore, had been seriously beaten; news reached the camp that he had been killed. On the night of August 23 the city of Houston was shot up; two Negroes and seventeen white people were killed, five of the latter being Houston policemen. As a result, sixty-three members of the battalion were court-martialled at Fort Sam Houston, and, on December 11, 1917, thirteen of them were hanged. A wave of bitterness and anguish, made more acute by a sense of impotence, swept over the coloured people. They did not question the findings of the court martial, but they did feel that the men should have been accorded their right of appeal to their Commander-in-Chief, the President. And they knew so well the devilish and fiendish baiting by which the men had been goaded.

A second court martial sentenced five more to be hanged and in addition sentenced fifty-one to life imprisonment and five to long terms. At this point a committee of four representatives from the National Association for the Advancement of Colored People—the Rev. George Frazier Miller, the Rev. Frank M. Hyder, the Rev. F. A. Cullen, and James Weldon Johnson, secretary of the association—proceeded from New York to Washington to see President Wilson, taking with them a petition signed by twelve thousand New York citizens asking executive clemency for the condemned men. Mr. Johnson acted as spokesman and in presenting the petition said:

"We come as a delegation from the New York Branch of the National Association for the Advancement of Colored People, representing the twelve thousand signers to this petition which we have the honour to lay before you. And we come not only as the representatives of those who signed this petition, but we come representing the sentiments and aspirations and sorrows, too, of the great mass of the Negro population of the United States.

"We respectfully and earnestly request and urge that you extend executive clemency to the five Negro soldiers of the Twenty-fourth Infantry now under sentence of death by court martial. And understanding that the cases of the men of the same regiment who were sentenced to life imprisonment by the first court martial are to be reviewed, we also request and urge that you cause this review to be laid before you and that executive clemency be shown also to them.

"We feel that the history of this particular regiment and the splendid record for bravery and loyalty of our Negro soldiery in every crisis of the nation give us the right to make this request. And we make it not only in the name of their loyalty, but also in the name of the unquestioned loyalty to the nation of twelve million Negroes—a loyalty which today places them side by side with the original American stocks that landed at Plymouth and Jamestown.

"The hanging of thirteen men without the opportunity of appeal to the Secretary of War or to their Commander-in-Chief, the President of the United States, was a punishment so drastic and so unusual in the history of the nation that the execution of additional members of the Twenty-fourth

Infantry would to the coloured people of the country savour of vengeance rather than justice.

"It is neither our purpose nor is this the occasion to argue whether this attitude of mind on the part of coloured people is justified or not. As representatives of the race we desire only to testify that it does exist. This state of mind has been intensified by the significant fact that although white persons were involved in the Houston affair, and the regiment to which the coloured men belonged was officered entirely by white men, none but coloured men, so far as we have been able to learn, have been prosecuted or condemned.

"We desire also respectfully to call to your attention the fact that there were mitigating circumstances for the action of these men of the Twenty-fourth Infantry. Not by any premeditated design and without cause did these men do what they did at Houston; but by a long series of humiliating and harassing incidents, culminating in the brutal assault on Corporal Baltimore, they were goaded to sudden and frenzied action. This is borne out by the long record for orderly and soldierly conduct on the part of the regiment throughout its whole history up to that time.

"And to the end that you extend the clemency which we ask, we lay before you this petition signed by white as well as coloured citizens of New York; one of the signers being a white man, president of a New York bank, seventy-two years of age, and a native of Lexington, Kentucky.

"And now, Mr. President, we would not let this opportunity pass without mentioning the terrible outrages against our people that have taken place in the last three-quarters of a year; outrages that are not only unspeakable wrongs against them, but blots upon the fair name of our common country. We mention the riots at East St. Louis, in which the coloured people bore the brunt of both the cruelty of the mob and the processes of law. And we especially mention the savage burnings that have taken place in the single state of Tennessee within nine months: the burnings at Memphis, Tennessee; at Dyersburg, Tennessee; and only last week at Estill Springs, Tennessee, where a Negro charged with the killing of two men was tortured with red-hot irons, then saturated with oil and burned to death before a crowd of American men, women, and children. And we ask that you, who have spoken so nobly to the whole world for the cause of humanity, speak against these specific wrongs. We realize that your high position and the tremendous moral influence which you wield in the world will give a word from you greater force than could come from any other source. Our people are intently listening and praying that you may find it in your heart to speak that word."

The President received the delegation very cordially and granted them an audience lasting half an hour. He assured them, in effect, that he would carefully examine the record in the case of the condemned men and would give the whole matter his sympathetic attention. A surprising incident of the interview was that the President declared that he had not heard anything about the Estill Springs burning. He asked the committee to state the facts for him. His comment was that he could hardly believe that such a thing had happened in the United States. He promised to seek an opportunity and later he did make a strong statement against lynching.

President Wilson prohibited the execution of any more American soldiers—except in General Pershing's forces abroad—before the sentences of the courts martial had been reviewed by the War Department. Eleven more men of the Twenty-fourth, making sixteen, were condemned to die. The President, after review of their cases, commuted ten death-sentences and affirmed six. The men who were sent to prison finally had their sentences commuted and were released on parole through the efforts of the Advancement Association.

Exactly what happened at Houston on that night in August will probably never be known. The executed men went to death and the fifty-odd to prison without "talking." According to the military investigation that was made, Bartlett James, one of the white officers, a West Pointer and a splendid soldier, Captain of Company L, was in the company street that night with his men gathered round him; a detail from the men who had left camp came back to induce the rest of the battalion to join them; the corporal in charge of the detail is said to have appealed to the men of Company L to follow, but none made a move; in reply to an appeal to him, Captain James was reported as saying: "The men of Company L are going to stay with their captain"; and he did hold his company practically intact. Captain James was down as one of the most important witnesses in this remarkable military trial. But on Wednesday night, October 24, seven days before the date set for the trial to begin, he went to his tent and blew out his brains. So the one officer of the line who could have told a great deal about the matter did not testify.

These were some of the depressing happenings at home after our entry into the war. From the other side came tidings far from being glad. There came back reports of the practices of discrimination and "Jim Crowism" against Negro soldiers; of the efforts to belittle and discredit their fighting qualities; of the ceaseless endeavours at every turn on the part of many of the white American troops to create a prejudice against them where none had existed. By one means or another, copies of the order entitled "Secret Information Concerning Black American Troops" found their way from France into the United States. This order, issued at the instance of American authorities and through the French military mission, was for the instruction of French officers in dealing with American Negro troops. It deprecated any intimacy between French officers and black officers. Specifically it said: "We may be courteous and amiable with these last, but we cannot deal with them on the same plane as with the white American officers without deeply wounding the latter. We must not eat with them, must not shake hands or seek to talk or meet with them outside of the requirements of the military service." Regarding credit for what the black American troops might accomplish through their courage or sacrifice, the order said: "We must not commend too highly the black American troops, particularly in the presence of (white) Americans. It is all right to recognize their good qualities and their services, but only in moderate terms, strictly in keeping with the truth." Out of such an order the great taboo could not be left: "Make a point of keeping the native cantonment population from 'spoiling' the Negroes. (White) Americans become greatly incensed at any public expression of intimacy between white women and black men." All these "dont's" had a familiar, homelike ring. Their origin and authenticity could not be doubted.

With the close of the war went most of the illusions and high hopes American Negroes had felt would be realized when it was seen that they were doing to the utmost their bit at home and in the field. Eight months after the armistice, with black men back fresh from the front, there broke the Red Summer of 1919, and the mingled emotions of the race were bitterness, despair, and anger. There developed an attitude of cynicism that was a characteristic foreign to the Negro. There developed also a spirit of defiance bom of desperation. These sentiments and reactions found varying degrees of expression in the Negro publications throughout the country; but Harlem became the centre where they were formulated and voiced to the Negroes of America and the world. Radicalism in Harlem, which had declined as the war approached, burst out anew. But it was something different from the formal radicalism of pre-war days; it was a radicalism motivated by a fierce race consciousness.

A new radical press sprang up in Harlem, and those periodicals that were older took on fresh vigour. Among the magazines and newspapers published were: *The Messenger, Challenge, The Voice, The Crusader, The Emancipator,* and *The Negro World.* These periodicals were edited and written by men who had a remarkable command of forcible and trenchant English, the precise style for their purpose. And the group was not at all a small one; in it were: A. Philip Randolph, Chandler Owen, George Frazier Miller, W. A. Domingo, Edgar M. Grey, Hubert Harrison, William H. Ferris, William Bridges, Richard B. Moore, Cyril V. Briggs, William N. Colson, and Anselmo Jackson. Two of these men, A. Philip Randolph and W. A. Domingo, wrote in a very close-knit, cogent manner. The utterances of these publications drew the notice of the Federal Government, and under the caption "Radicalism and Sedition among the Negroes as Reflected in their Publications" they were cited in a Department of Justice report made by Attorney General Palmer in 1919. The report of the Lusk Committee in New York State devoted forty-four pages to them. The radicalism of these publications ranged from left centre to extreme left; at the extreme it was submerged in what might be called racialism. It was to be expected that at such a time an organization like the National Association for the Advancement of Colored People would not escape scrutiny. The utterances of Dr. Du Bois in the *Crisis*, the organ of the association, brought a visit to the office from agents of the Department of Justice. In reply to the query: "Just what is this organization fighting for?" Dr. Du Bois said: "We are fighting for the enforcement of the Constitution of the United States." This was an ultimate condensation of the program of the association.

The Messenger preached socialism and the social revolution. It was the most widely circulated of all the radical periodicals and probably the most influential. In an editorial, "The Cause of and Remedy for Race Riots," it said in part:

> The solution will not follow the meeting of white and Negro leaders in love feasts, who pretend, like the African ostrich, that nothing is wrong, because their heads are buried in the sand.
>
> On the economic field, industry must be socialized, and land must be nationalized, which will thereby remove the motive for creating strife between the races. . . .
>
> The people must organize, own and control their press.
>
> The church must be converted into an educational forum.
>
> The stage and screen must be controlled by the people.

This editorial offered an "immediate program," which was summed up in the following paragraph:

> *Lastly, revolution must come.* By that we mean a complete change in the organization of society. Just as absence of

industrial democracy is productive of riots and race clashes, so the introduction of industrial democracy will be the longest step toward removing that cause. When no profits are to be made from race friction, no one will longer be interested in stirring up race prejudice. The quickest way to stop a thing or to destroy an institution is to destroy the profitableness of that institution. The capitalist system must go and its going must be hastened by the workers themselves.

Challenge was, perhaps, the least restrained of the radical publications. It had no theory of reform like the *Messenger*. It made a direct appeal to the emotions. It assaulted, not the class-line, but the colour-line; and so spoke a language that the great majority understood. Its editor, William Bridges, was master of a rhythmic, impassioned prose that possessed the power of stirring masses of people. In the use of this sort of instrument he has been surpassed by few, if any, pamphleteering champions of a cause in this country. In one of his editorials, in which he sought to bring about a union of forces and a united front on the part of American Negroes and West Indians, he said:

There is no West Indian slave, no American slave; you are all slaves, base, ignoble slaves.

There is no more love in the hearts of the British statesmen when passing laws to curtail the liberties of their black subject than there is in the hearts of Americans when passing similar laws to abridge the liberties of theirs.

West Indian Negroes, you are oppressed. American Negroes, you are equally oppressed. West Indians, you are black. Americans, you are equally black. It is your color upon which white men pass judgment, not your merits, nor the geographical line between you. Stretch hands across the seas, with the immortal cry of Patrick Henry: "Give me Liberty or Give me Death."

Prayer will not do all. White men expect to keep you in eternal slavery through superstitions that they have long cast off. They delight in seeing you on your knees. They mean to remain on their feet. They want your eyes kept on the gold in heaven. They mean to keep their eyes on the gold of the world. They want you to seek rest beyond the grave. They mean to have all the rest this side of it.

Can't you see that with every tick of the clock and every revolution of the eternal sun your chains are fastened tighter? You are cursed with superstition and ignorance. You are not taught to love Frederick Douglass, L'Ouverture, Dessalines, and Tubman. You are always taught to love George Washington, Wm. Pitt, Abraham Lincoln, and Wm. Gladstone. . . .

West Indians, the only things you are wanted and permitted to do that white men do is worship the king and sing "Britannia Rules the Waves," no matter if Britannia rules you more sternly than she ever does the waves.

Americans, the only thing that you are wanted and are permitted to do that white men do is to be loyal and sing, "The Star Spangled Banner," no matter how many Southern hillsides are spangled with the blood of many another innocent Negro. . . .

Negroes of the West Indies and America, Unite! Slavery is just as bad under a king as under a president. We don't want white wives; we don't want to dine in the homes of white men; we don't want the things they have acquired; but by the eternal God that reigns on high listen to the rhythmic voice of the New Negro ringing at the court gates of kings and presidents like a raging tempest wind, furious as a curse of Hell, valorous, determined, unafraid, crying: "Give Us Liberty or Give Us Death."

In each issue of the magazine there was printed "An Oath," which the report of the Lusk Committee listed as "another typical example of inflammatory propaganda." The oath read:

> BY ETERNAL HEAVEN—
>
> I swear never to love any flag simply for its color, nor any country for its name.
>
> The flag of my affections must rest over me as a banner of protection, not as a sable shroud.
>
> The country of my patriotism must be above color distinctions, must be one of laws, not of men; of law and not lawlessness, of LIBERTY and not BONDAGE, of privilege to all, not special privilege to some.
>
> Kaiser is not the only word synonymous with IMPERIALISM, TYRANNY, MURDER, and RAPINE.
>
> PRESIDENT AND KING are not the only words synonymous with DEMOCRACY, FREEDOM, PROGRESS.
>
> I shall love not names but deeds. I shall pay homage to any and all men who strive to rid the world of the pestilential diseases of WAR, PREJUDICE, OPPRESSION, LYNCHING.
>
> I am a Patriot.

I am not merely of a Race and a Country, but of the World.

I am BROTHERHOOD.

These journals shook up the Negroes of New York and the country and effected some changes that have not been lost; but able as were most of the men behind them, as radicals, they failed almost wholly in bringing about any co-ordination of the forces they were dealing with; perhaps that was to be expected. This post-war radical movement gradually waned—as it waned among whites—and the organs of the movement, one by one, withered and died. The *Messenger*, which continued to be published up to last year, was the longest-lived of them all. *The Negro World* is still being published; but it falls in a classification distinctly its own.

The Harlem radicals failed to bring about a correlation of the forces they had called into action, to have those forces work through a practical medium to a definite objective; but they did much to prepare the ground for a man who could and did do that, a man who was one of the most remarkable and picturesque figures that have appeared on the American scene—Marcus Garvey.

Marcus Garvey is a full-blooded black man, bom, and bom poor, in Jamaica, British West Indies, in 1887. He grew up under the triple race scheme that prevails in many of the West Indian islands—white, mulatto, and black. The conditions of this system aroused in him, even as a boy, a deep resentment, which increased as he grew older. His resentment against the mulattos was, perhaps, deeper than his resentment against the whites. At about the time he became of age, he left Jamaica and travelled in South America. He next went to England, where he stayed for several years. All the while he was seeking some escape from the terrible pressure of the colour bar. In England he met one or two African agitators. He became intimate with Duse Muhamed Effendi, an African political writer, who was running a small revolutionary newspaper in London, and from him learned something about world politics, especially with relation to Africa. It was probably then that he began to dream of a land where black men ruled. England was a disappointment. In 1914 he returned to Jamaica, determined to do something to raise the status of the black masses of the island. He began his public career by organizing the Universal Negro Improvement Association. He was discouraged by the fact that he aroused more interest and gained more support among the whites than among the blacks. He wrote Booker T. Washington about his plans—plans probably for establishing industrial training for the natives of Jamaica—and received a reply encouraging him to come to the United States. Before he could perfect arrangements to come, Booker T. Washington had died. But on March 23, 1916 Garvey landed in Harlem.

In some way or other he got about the country, visiting, as he says, thirty-eight states, studying the condition of the Negro in America, and then returned to New York. On June 12, 1917 a large mass meeting, called by Hubert Harrison, was held in Bethel A. M. E. Church in Harlem for the purpose of organizing the Liberty League. Some two thousand people were present, and among them was Marcus Garvey. Mr. Harrison introduced him to the audience and asked him to say a few words. This was Harlem's first real sight of Garvey, and his first real chance at Harlem. The man spoke, and his magnetic personality, torrential eloquence, and intuitive knowledge of crowd psychology were all brought into play. He swept the audience along with him. He made his speech an endorsement of the new movement and a pledge of his hearty support of it; but Garvey was not of the kidney to support anybody's movement. He had seen the United States and he had seen Harlem. He had doubtless been the keenest observer at the Liberty League organization meeting; and it may be that it was then he decided upon New York as the centre for his activities.

He soon organized and incorporated the Universal Negro Improvement Association in the United States, with New York as headquarters. He made his first appeal to the West Indian elements, not only to British, but to Spanish and French, and they flocked to him. He established the *Negro World* as his organ and included in it Spanish and French sections. He built Liberty Hall, a great basement that held five or six thousand people. There the association held its first convention in 1919, during the whole month of August, with delegates from the various states and the West Indies. By this time the scheme of the organization had expanded from the idea of economic solution of the race problem through the establishment of "Universal" shops and factories and financial institutions to that of its solution through the redemption of Africa and the establishment of a Negro merchant marine. At the mass meeting held in Carnegie Hall during this convention, Garvey in his address said:

> "We are striking homeward toward Africa to make her the big black republic. And in the making of Africa the big black republic, what is the barrier? The barrier is the white man; and we say to the white man who dominates Africa that it is to his interest to clear out now, because we are coming, not as in the time of Father Abraham, 200,000 strong, but we are coming 400,000,000 strong and we mean to retake every square inch of the 12,000,000 square miles of African territory belonging to us by right Divine."

Money poured in; wartime prosperity made it possible. Three ships were bought and placed in commission. Garvey had grown to be High Potentate of the association and "Provisional President of Africa." Around him he had established a court of nobles and ladies. There were dukes and duchesses, knight commanders of the Distinguished Order of Ethiopia, and knight commanders of the Sublime Order of the Nile. There were gorgeous uniforms, regalia, decorations, and insignia. There was a strict court etiquette, and the constitution provided that "No lady below the age of eighteen shall be presented at the 'Court Reception' and no gentleman below the age of twenty-one." There was established the African Legion, with a full line of commissioned officers and a quartermaster staff and commissariat for each brigade. The Black Cross nurses were organized. In fact, an embryo army was set up with Marcus Garvey as commander-in-chief. A mission was sent to Liberia to negotiate an agreement whereby the Universal Improvement Association would establish a colony there and aid in the development of the country.

Garvey became a world figure, and his movements and utterances were watched by the great governmental powers. (Even today from his exile in Jamaica his actions and words are considered international news.) The U. N. I. A. grew in the United States and spread through the region of the Caribbean. The movement became more than a movement, it became a religion, its members became zealots. Meetings at Liberty Hall were conducted with an elaborate liturgy. The moment for the entry of the "Provisional President" into the auditorium was solemn; a hushed and expectant silence on the throng, the African Legion and Black Cross nurses flanking the long aisle and coming to attention, the band and audience joining in the hymn: "Long Live our President," and Garvey, surrounded by his guard of honour from the Legion, marching majestically through the double line and mounting the rostrum; it was impressive if for no other reason than the way in which it impressed the throng. Garvey made a four months' tour of the West Indies in a Black Star liner, gathering in many converts to the movement, but no freight for the vessel. Of course, the bubble burst. Neither Garvey nor anyone with him knew how to operate ships. And if they had known, they could not have succeeded at the very time when ships were the greatest drug on the market. So the Black Star Line, after swallowing up hundreds of thousands of dollars, collapsed in December 1921. The Federal Government investigated Garvey's share-selling scheme and he was indicted and convicted on a charge of using the mails to defraud. While out of the Tombs on bail, he made an unsuccessful attempt to revive his shipping venture as the Black Cross Line.

Within ten years after reaching New York Marcus Garvey had risen and fallen, been made a prisoner in the Atlanta Federal Penitentiary, and finally been deported to his native island. Within that brief period a black West Indian, here in the United States, in the twentieth century, had actually played an imperial role such as Eugene O'Neill never imagined in his *Emperor Jones*.

Garvey failed; yet he might have succeeded with more than moderate success. He had energy and daring and the Napoleonic personality, the personality that draws masses of followers. He stirred the imagination of the Negro masses as no Negro ever had. He raised more money in a few years than any other Negro organization had ever dreamed of. He had great power and great possibilities within his grasp. But his deficiencies as a leader outweighed his abilities. He is a supreme egotist, his egotism amounting to megalomania; and so the men surrounding him had to be for the most part cringing sycophants; and among them there were also cunning knaves. Upon them he now lays the entire blame for failure, taking no part of it to himself. As he grew in power, he fought every other Negro rights organization in the country, especially the National Association for the Advancement of Colored People, centring his attacks upon Dr. Du Bois.

Garvey made several vital blunders, which, with any intelligent advice, he might have avoided. He proceeded upon the assumption of a triple race scheme in the United States; whereas the facts are that the whites in the United States, unlike the whites of the West Indies, make no distinction between people of colour and blacks, nor do the Negroes. There may be places where a very flexible social line exists, but Negroes in the United States of every complexion have always maintained a solid front on the rights of the race. This policy of Garvey, going to the logical limit of calling upon his followers to conceive of God as black, did arouse a latent pride of the Negro in his blackness, but it wrought an overbalancing damage by the effort to drive a wedge between the blacks and the mixed bloods, an effort that might have brought on disaster had it been more successful.

He made the mistake of ignoring or looking with disdain upon the technique of the American Negro in dealing with his problems of race, a technique acquired through three hundred years of such experience as the West Indian has not had and never can have. If he had availed himself of the counsel and advice of an able and honest American Negro, he would have avoided many of the barbed wires against which he ran and many of the pits into which he fell.

But the main reason for Garvey's failure with thoughtful American Negroes was his African scheme. It was recognized at once by them to be impracticable and fantastic. Indeed, it is difficult to give the man credit for either honesty or sanity in these imperialistic designs, unless, as there are some reasons to suppose, his designs involved the purpose of going into Liberia as an agent of development and then by gradual steps or a coup taking over the government and making the country the centre of the activities and efforts for an Africa Redeemed. But thoughtful coloured Americans knew that, under existing political conditions in Africa, even that plan could ultimately meet with nothing but failure. Had there been every prospect of success, however, the scheme would not have appealed to them. It was simply a restatement of the Colonization Society scheme advanced just one hundred years before, which had occasioned the assembling of the first national convention of Negroes in America, called to oppose "the operations and misrepresentations of the American Colonization Society in these United States." The central idea of Garvey's scheme was absolute abdication and the recognition as facts of the assertions that this is a white man's country, a country in which the Negro has no place, no right, no chance, no future. To that idea the overwhelming majority of thoughtful American Negroes will not subscribe. And behind this attitude is the common-sense realization that as the world is at present, the United States, with all of its limitations, offers the millions of Negroes within its borders greater opportunities than any other land.

Garvey's last great mistake came about through his transcending egotism. He had as leading counsel for his trial Henry Lincoln Johnson, one of the shrewdest and ablest Negro lawyers in the country. But the temptation to strut and pose before a crowded court and on the front pages of the New York newspapers was too great for Garvey to resist; so he brushed his lawyers aside and handled his own case. He himself examined and cross-examined the witnesses; he himself harangued the judge and jury; and he was convicted.

Garvey, practically exiled on an island in the Caribbean, becomes a somewhat tragic figure. There arises a slight analogy between him and that former and greater dreamer in empires, exiled on another island. But the heart of the tragedy is that to this man came an opportunity such as comes to few men, and he clutched greedily at the glitter and let the substance slip from his fingers.

NINETEEN

T HE MOST OUTSTANDING PHASE OF THE development of the Negro in the United States during the past decade has been the recent literary and artistic emergence of the individual creative artist; and New York has been, almost exclusively, the place where that emergence has taken place. The thing that has happened has been so marked that it does not have the appearance of a development; it seems rather like a sudden awakening, like an instantaneous change. The story of it, as of almost every experience relating to the Negro in America, goes back a long way. For many generations the Negro has been a creative artist and a contributor to the nation's common cultural store. Underlying all these contributions are his folk-art creations—his sacred music: the Spirituals; his secular music: the plantation songs, rag-time, blues, jazz, and the work songs; his folk-lore: the Uncle Remus stories and other plantation tales; and his dances. All of these have gone into and, more or less, permeated our national life. Some of them, various THE MOST outstanding phase of the development of the Negro in the United States during the past decade has been the recent literary and artistic emergence of the individual creative artist; and New York has been, almost exclusively, the place where that emergence has taken place. The thing that has happened has been so marked that it does not have the appearance of a development; it seems rather like a sudden awakening, like an instantaneous change. The story of it, as of almost every experience relating to the Negro in America, goes back a long way. For many generations the Negro has been a creative artist and a contributor to the nation's common cultural store. Underlying all these contributions are his folk-art creations—his sacred music: the Spirituals; his secular music: the plantation songs, rag-time, blues, jazz, and the work songs; his folk-lore: the Uncle Remus stories and other plantation tales; and his dances. All of these have gone into and, more or less, permeated our national life. Some of them, various forms of his secular music and his dances, have been completely taken over; they are no longer racial, they are wholly national. Even the Uncle Remus stories have been appropriated and appear, with slight adaptations, in the daily newspapers as popular bedtime stories.

But the individual creative artist is not entirely new. The actual record goes back for more than two hundred and fifty years. In the books it is usually set down as beginning with Phillis Wheatley. Phillis Wheatley was born in Africa. When she was eight or nine years old, in 1761, she was landed in Boston from a slave-ship. Mr. Wheatley, a philanthropic Boston gentleman, purchased her as a maid for his wife. Phillis was given an education, and in 1773 she published a volume of poems. Her book was the second volume of poems published by a woman in America. It is needless to say that Phillis Wheatley is not a great American poet—in her day there were no great American poets—but judged alongside her contemporaries, she is one of America's important poets. The thread of the story can be traced farther back, however, and when it is, it leads to New York. The first Negro in America to write and publish poems was Jupiter Hammon, a slave belonging to a Mr. Lloyd of Queens Village, Long Island. Hammon's poems were published in broadside form and had a rather popular circulation for ten or fifteen years. His first poem appeared in 1760 and was entitled *An Evening Thought, Salvation by Christ, with Pennettential Cries.* In 1788 he published *An Address to Miss Phillis Wheatley, Ethiopian Poetess in Boston, who came from Africa at eight years of age, and soon became acquainted with the Gospel of Jesus Christ.* All of Hammon's poems were religious in tone; it is likely that he was a preacher. In distinction, Phillis Wheatley was a classicist and wrote strictly in the form and style of Alexander Pope. Jupiter Hammon was also a man interested in affairs. Before the New York African Society, a Negro organization in Manhattan, he read, in 1784, a paper entitled *An Address to the Negroes in the State of New York.* The address was printed in 1787. Four hundred and fifty dollars was paid for a copy of it for the collection of the late J. Pierpont Morgan. It is interesting to know that the New York African Society is still an active organization.

Few Americans, even the well informed, know anything about Jupiter Hammon. More, of course, know about Phillis Wheatley. And a great many more know about Paul Laurence Dunbar. But it is probable that very few indeed know that between Phillis Wheatley and Paul Laurence Dunbar (who died in 1906) there were thirty-odd Negroes who published volumes of verse. Within the same period there were hundreds of pamphleteers, essayists, and authors of books of various kinds. Of this work, some was good, most was mediocre, and much was bad—and practically all of it unknown to the general public. The seeming suddenness of the emergence of the Negro in literature is mainly due to the fact that by the work of the Harlem group of writers America at large has, in a very brief time, been made aware that there are Negro authors with something interesting to say and the skill to say it. It was the quickness with which this awareness was brought about that gave the movement the aspect of a phenomenon.

Towards the close of the World War there sprang up a group of eight or ten poets in various cities of the country who sang a newer song. The group discarded traditional dialect and the stereotyped material of Negro poetry. Its members did not concern themselves with the sound of the old banjo and the singing round the cabin door; nor with the successions of the watermelon, possum, and sweet potato seasons. They broke away entirely from the limitations of pathos and humour. Also they broke away from use of the subject material that had already been over-used by white American poets of a former generation. What they did was to attempt to express what the masses of their race were then feeling and thinking and wanting to hear. They attempted to make those masses articulate. And so the distinguishing notes of their poetry were disillusionment, protest, and challenge—and sometimes despair. And they created, each in accordance with his talent and power, authentic poetry. The poems of the Negro poets of the immediate post-war period were widely printed in Negro publications; they were committed to memory; they were recited at school exercises and public meetings and were discussed at private gatherings. These revolutionary poets made black America fully aware of them.

But there was among them a voice too powerful to be confined to the circle of race, a voice that carried further and made America in general aware; it was that of Claude McKay, of the Harlem group. Here was a true poet of great skill and wide range, who turned from creating the mood of poetic beauty in the absolute, as he had so fully done in such poems as *The Harlem Dancer* and *Flame Heart*, for example, and began pouring out cynicism, bitterness, and invective. For this purpose, incongruous as it may seem, he took the sonnet form as his medium. There is nothing in American literature that strikes a more portentous note than these sonnet-tragedies of McKay. Here is the sestet of his sonnet "The Lynching":[1]

> Day dawned, and soon the mixed crowds came to view
> The ghastly body swaying in the sun:
> The women thronged to look, but never a one
> Showed sorrow in her eyes of steely blue;
> And little lads, lynchers that were to be,
> Danced round the dreadful thing in fiendish glee.

The red summer of 1919 brought from McKay this cry of defiant despair, sounded from the last ditch:

> If we must die let it be not like hogs Hunted and penned in
> an inglorious spot. . . .
> O kinsmen! We must meet the common foe!
> Though far outnumbered, let us show us brave,
> And for their thousand blows deal one death-blow!
> What though before us lies the open grave?
> Like men we'll face the murderous, cowardly pack, Pressed
> to the wall, dying, but fighting back!

But not all the terror of the time could smother the poet of beauty and universality in McKay. In America, which opens with these lines,

> Although she feeds me bread of bitterness,
> And sinks into my throat her tiger's tooth,

1. Quotations from Claude McKay's poetry are from his *Harlem Shadows*, copyright 1922, by Harcsourt, Brace and Company, Inc., New York.

Stealing my breath of life, I will confess I love this cultured
hell that tests my youth!

he fused these elements of fear and bitterness and hate into verse which
by every test is true poetry and a fine sonnet. Reading McKay's poetry
of rebellion it is difficult to conceive of him dreaming of his native
Jamaica and singing:

So much have I forgotten in ten years,
So much in ten brief years! I have forgot
What time the purple apples come to juice,
And what month brings the shy forget-me-not.
I have forgot the special, startling season
Of the pimento's flowering and fruiting;
What time of year the ground doves brown the fields
And fill the noonday with their curious fluting.
I have forgotten much, hut still remember
The poinsettia's red, blood-red in warm December.

Mr. McKay was bom in Jamaica, British West Indies, in 1890. He
came to the United States when he was twenty-one years of age, having
already published a volume of verse, *Songs of Jamaica*. He first attracted
attention here by two sonnets published in the *Seven Arts* under the
name Eli Edwards. What perverse whim could have suggested to a poet
named Claude McKay the use of such a pseudonym? Later his work
appeared in other magazines, principally in the *Liberator*. He published
Harlem Shadows in 1922. Claude McKay's poetry was one of the
great forces in bringing about what is often called the "Negro literary
renaissance." But he is now almost silent as a poet.

In 1922 *The Book of American Negro Poetry*, edited by James Weldon Johnson, was published. This anthology contained an essay on "The Negro's Creative Genius" by the editor, and presented to the general reading public a representative collection of poetry by American Negroes from the earliest writers down to and including that written by Negro poets immediately following the World War. The book was effective in following up the work of making America at large aware.

Within five or six years after the close of the war there had sprung up a group of younger Negro poets. Like the immediate post-war group, they were scattered in different cities. Of these younger poets there were some fifteen writing verse of distinction; and four-fifths of that number belonged either to New York or to Washington. Two of the poets belonging to the Harlem group rose above the level and gained, almost simultaneously, a recognition for themselves which carried the Negro literary movement far forward and succeeded greatly in focusing national attention upon it. These two poets were Countee Cullen, born in New York in 1903, and Langston Hughes, born in Joplin, Missouri, in 1902.

The rise of the post-war poets was a revolt against the sentimentality and imploration that had preceded them. The rise of the younger poets was a revolt against the "propaganda" of the post-war group. The younger group made a natural attempt to get from under the weight that "race" put upon their art. Some of them sought escape by feigning to ignore absolutely the barriers with which "race" hedged them about. This process of auto-hypnosis often resulted in poetry of bravado or, worse, of bombast. It is interesting to note how Cullen and Hughes handled this incubus, for neither of them has escaped "race."

Mr. Cullen may with justification chafe under any limitation of art to race, for he is a true lyric poet, a younger brother to Housman. And yet, in my opinion, the best of his poetry rises out of the idea of race and is permeated with it. But it is through his ability suddenly to deepen and heighten these very experiences that his race-conscious poetry becomes the thing of beauty, at times almost insufferable beauty, that it is; it is through this ability that he achieves some of his finest effects. One dares to say that the two most poignant lines in American literature are in a sonnet in which he speaks of the mysteries and paradoxes of life and expresses his faith that God can solve and answer them all, then pours into the final couplet an infinity of irony and bitterness, and pathos and tragedy:[2]

> Yet do I marvel at this curious thing:
> To make a poet black, and bid him sing!

Or take Mr. Cullen's "Heritage," one of his longer poems, one so dynamically charged with the experiences of race that it quivers. I do not think there is such compelling power and beauty in any purely white poem he has written. A part of the poem is sufficient to demonstrate its quality:

> What is Africa to me:
> Copper sun or scarlet sea,
> Jungle star or jungle track,
> Strong bronzed men, or regal black
> Women from whose loins I sprang
> When the birds of Eden sang?

---

2. The quotations from Countee Cullen's poetry are from *Color* (New York: Harper and Brothers, 1925).

One three centuries removed
From the scenes his fathers loved,
Spicy grove, cinnamon tree,
What is Africa to me?

So I lie, who all day long
Want no sound except the song
Sung by wild barbaric birds
Goading massive jungle herds,
Juggernauts of flesh that pass
Trampling tall defiant grass
Where young forest lovers lie,
Plighting troth beneath the sky.
So I lie, who always hear,
Though I cram against my ear
Both my thumbs, and keep them there,
Great drums throbbing through the air.
So I lie, whose font of pride,
Dear distress, and joy allied,
Is my sombre flesh and skin,
With the dark blood dammed within
Like great pulsing tides of wine
That, I fear, must burst the fine
Channels of the chafing net
Where they surge and foam and fret. .

Quaint, outlandish heathen gods
Black men fashion out of rods,
Clay, and brittle bits of stone,
In a likeness like their own,

My conversion came high-priced;
I belong to Jesus Christ,
Preacher of humility;
Heathen gods are naught to me.

Father, Son, and Holy Ghost,
So I make an idle boast;
Jesus of the twice turned cheek,
Lamb of God, although I speak
With my mouth thus, in my heart
Do I play a double part.
Ever at Thy glowing altar
Must my heart grow sick and falter,
Wishing He I served were black,
Thinking then it would not lack
Precedent of pain to guide it,
Let who would or might deride it;
Surely then this flesh would know
Yours had borne a kindred woe.
Lord, I fashion dark gods, too,
Daring even to give you
Dark despairing features where,
Crowned with dark rebellious hair,
Patience wavers just so much as
Mortal grief compels, while touches
Quick and hot, of anger, rise
To smitten cheek and weary eyes.
Lord, forgive me if my need
Sometimes shapes a human creed.

·

All day long and all night through,
One thing only must I do:
Quench my pride and cool my blood,
Lest I perish in the flood.
Lest a hidden ember set
Timber that I thought was wet
Burning like the dryest flax,
Melting like the merest wax,
Lest the grave restore its dead.
Not yet has my heart or head
In the least way realized
They and I are civilized.

Even when he turns to humour, Mr. Cullen distills his best brand from the idea of race. Good illustrations are his "Baltimore Incident" and his epitaph "For a Lady I Know":

She even thinks that up in heaven
    Her class lies late and snores,
While poor black cherubs rise at seven
    To do celestial chores.

Mr. Cullen published his first volume of poems, *Color*, in 1925, when he was twenty-two; the book placed him at once in the list of American poets. He has followed it with *The Ballad of the Brown Girl*, *Copper Sun*, *Caroling Dusk*, an anthology of verse by Negro poets from Paul Laurence Dunbar down to and including the younger group, and *The Black Christ*, a long narrative poem.

Langston Hughes is a cosmopolite. Young as he is, he has been over most of the world, making his own way. Consciously he snaps his fingers at race, as he does at a great many other things. He belongs to the line of rebel poets. He is a rebel not only in the matter of poetic form, but also in the choice of poetic subjects, for, of subjects, he is as likely to take one from the gutter as from any other place. On this point he has met with the disapprobation and censure of some in his own race who feel that the subject-matter of his poems is not sufficiently elevating. Yet Mr. Hughes, too, falls under this idea of race, and most of his best work springs from it. It is by taking this idea and shooting it through with a cynicism and a sardonic humour peculiarly his own that he secures some of his finest effects. These effects are very unlike Mr. Cullen's, but have a quality of equal finality.

Mr. Hughes writes a poem which has for its title and its subject "Brass Spittoons." Here, if ever there was one, is an "unpoetic" subject. But the poet takes it and tells of the black porter at his distasteful task of cleaning brass spittoons; tells of him in Detroit, Chicago, Atlantic City, Palm Beach; cleaning spittoons in Pullman cars, clubs, and hotel lobbies; picking up nickels, dimes—and a dollar, two dollars a day. Then at the end he flashes back over an otherwise sordid poem these bright lines freighted with implications of "race":[3]

> Hey, boy!
> A bright bowl of brass is beautiful to the Lord. Bright polished
> brass like the cymbals Of King David's dancers,
> Like the wine cups of Solomon.
> Hey, boy!
> A clean spitoon on the altar of the Lord.

3. Quotations from Langston Hughes's poetry are taken from *The Weary Blues* and *Fine Clothes to the Jew* (New York: Alfred A. Knopf).

A clean bright spitoon all newly polished,—
At least I can offer that.

       Com' mere, Boy!

No matter how Mr. Hughes handles this idea of "race," he is very seldom sentimental and never pathetic. But this is not due to any flinty quality in his poetry. In much of his work the throb and the tear lie close to the surface. As a conscious artist he has in a large measure adopted the philosophy of the folk-bards, makers of the blues. That philosophy consists in choosing to laugh to keep from crying. Mr. Hughes might even subscribe to the philosophy summed up in that line in one of the blues:

Got de blues, an' too dam' mean to cry.

This is the chord played in *Mulatto* and many other of his poems. It is the chord that is struck in his poem *Cross*:

My old man's a white old man And my old mother's black.
If ever I cursed my white old man I take my curses back.
If ever I cursed my old black mother And wished she were
    in hell,
I'm sorry for that evil wish And now I wish her well.

My old man died in a fine big house.
My ma died in a shack.
I wonder where I'm gonna die,
Being neither white nor black?

But Hughes can also sing. In one of his poems he has the Negro speak of rivers:

I've known rivers:
I've known rivers ancient as the world and older than the
flow of human blood in human veins.

My soul has grown deep like the rivers.

I bathed in the Euphrates when dawns were young.
I built my hut near the Congo and it lulled me to sleep.
I looked upon the Nile and raised the pyramids above it.
I heard the singing of the Mississippi when Abe Lincoln went
down to New Orleans, and I've seen its muddy bosom
turn all golden in the sunset.

I've known rivers:
Ancient, dusky rivers.

My soul has grown deep like the rivers.

Mr. Hughes has published two volumes of poems: *The Weary Blues* in 1926, and *Fine Clothes to the Jew* in 1927. In the latter year *God's Trombones—Seven Negro Sermons in Verse*, by James Weldon Johnson, was published.

Early in the decade a fresh start was made in fiction. There had been the stories of Paul Laurence Dunbar and Charles W. Chesnutt. And later *The Quest of the Silver Fleece*, a novel by W. E. Burghardt Du

Bois, and *The Autobiography of an Ex-Coloured Man*, by James Weldon Johnson, appeared. In 1923 Jean Toomer published *Cane*, a string of stories of Negro life, interspersed with original lyrics. The book was in no degree a popular success, but it made a great impression on the critics. It is still often referred to as one of the finest pieces of modern American prose. The poems in the book stamp the author as a lyricist of the first order. Mr. Toomer was the prose pioneer in the work done in the past decade to make America in general aware of Negro artists and what they were doing; it is regrettable that he has written so little since.

In 1924 there appeared a novel that struck both the critics and the general public. It was the first piece of fiction written by an American Negro to accomplish this double feat with so large a degree of success. The book created a sensation and was the subject of heated controversy wherever it was discussed. It was *The Fire in the Flint* by Walter White. *The Fire in the Flint* was a realistic novel dealing in a fearless manner with the contemporary conditions surrounding Negro life in a small town in the South. Mr. White was well prepared to write such a book; he was born in Atlanta, Georgia, and educated at Atlanta University. In 1918 he came to New York to become assistant secretary of the National Association for the Advancement of Colored People. In that capacity he travelled through many parts of the South to make investigations of lynchings, race riots, and civil and social conditions among Negroes. Being a man who can be white or coloured as he may choose, he gathered a great deal of curious information. All of this experience he packed into this book and produced a story of extraordinary power. *The Fire in the Flint* was followed by *Flight*, a novel with "passing" as its theme. Last year Mr. White published *Rope and Faggot*, the most authoritative study of lynching yet made.

Just prior to *The Fire in the Flint*, a novel by Jessie Fauset, *There*

Is Confusion, made its appearance. Miss Fauset's book was a story of conditions surrounding contemporary Negro life in a Northern city. Her next novel was *Plum Bun*, a story with a similar theme. Until this decade of "literary renaissance" Negro writers had been less successful in fiction than in any other field they had tried. They had to their credit two remarkable autobiographies, several good historical works, some splendid collections of essays, a still larger number of collections of good poetry, and a great mass of volumes of polemical discussions on the race question. One could look back to only one good writer of fiction, Charles W. Chesnutt. But now, and for the first time, the output of fiction exceeded that of poetry. Within the past ten years more fiction has been published by Negro writers than had been brought out by them in the preceding two hundred and fifty years. And every bit of this fiction—that is, every bit that has been published in a way calculated to reach the general public— has been written by writers of the Harlem group. Nella Larsen published two well-written novels: one, *Quicksand*, the story of a coloured girl, with the scene laid in the South, in New York, and in Europe; and the other, *Passing*, a story of "passing." Eric Walrond published *Tropic Death*, a volume of colourful stories of West Indian and Panamanian life. Rudolph Fisher brought the first light, satirical touch in *The Walls of Jericho*. W. E. Burghardt Du Bois published *Dark Princess*, a novel that was fantasy and satire. Wallace Thurman published *The Blacker the Berry*. In 1927 *The Autobiography of an Ex-Coloured Man* was republished in New York. In 1928 Claude McKay broke his silence with a book of prose, *Home to Harlem*, a novel of life in Negro New York. This book appeared on the list of best sellers and was one of the successes of the season. McKay followed with another successful novel, *Banjo*. In 1929 Taylor Gordon published *Born to Be*, a story of his life, but at the same time containing, probably, an element of fiction. William Pickens published *Bursting*

Bonds, an autobiography, in 1923. Apart from fiction, but closely related to the literary and artistic movement, were the First and Second Books of *American Negro Spirituals,* edited and arranged by James Weldon and J. Rosamond Johnson, and published respectively in 1925 and 1926.

There are writers in Harlem who do a regular newspaper stint and contribute to the magazines; among them is George S. Schuyler, a brilliant writer and a first-class journalist and publicist. J. A. Rogers is another excellent newspaper and magazine contributor. The Negro novel of the World War is still unwritten.

In making America aware of the Negro artist and his work an important part was played by the Harlem Number (March 1925) of the *Survey Graphic.* This number of the Survey contained a hundred pages. There were twenty contributors, fifteen coloured and five white; twelve of the coloured contributors belonged to the Harlem group. Some of the articles were: "Enter the New Negro," "The Making of Harlem," "Black Workers and the City," "The Tropics in New York," "The Black Man Brings His Gifts," "Jazz at Home," "Negro Art and America," "The Negro Digs Up His Past," "The Rhythm of Harlem," "Color Lines," and "Ambushed in the City." There were also poems, drawings, and photographs. This issue of the *Survey* had the largest circulation of any in the history of the magazine up to that time; several editions had to be run off before the demand was satisfied. It was a revelation to New York and the country. Later the symposium, somewhat enlarged, was brought out as a book entitled *The New Negro,* under the editorship of Alain Locke. It remains one of the most important books on the Negro ever published.

Another decided impulse to the literary movement was furnished by the establishment in 1924 of cash prizes for original literary work. These prizes were offered through the two New York magazines, the

Crisis, organ of the National Association for the Advancement of Colored People, under the editorship of Dr. Du Bois, and *Opportunity*, the organ of the Urban League, under the editorship of Charles S. Johnson. The *Crisis* prizes were established through the generosity of Mrs. Amy E. Spingarn, and the *Opportunity* prizes through that of Mr. Caspar Holstein. Additional prizes were offered later by Carl Van Vechten through *Opportunity*, and by Carl Brandt through the *Crisis*. Also through the *Crisis* the Charles W. Chesnutt Honorarium was given. These prizes were given for several years and had quite a stimulating effect upon the younger writers. The title poem to Langston Hughes's first volume won an *Opportunity* prize.

In the other arts some advance, though not quite so marked, has been made in the decade just passed. In music the Harlem group has been a strong factor in giving a fresh interpretation and a new vogue to the Spirituals. The Spirituals have been sung before audiences for a long time. It has been sixty years since they were first introduced by the Fisk Jubilee Singers. But a change has been wrought in the reaction they call forth. Fifty years ago white people who heard the Spirituals sung were touched and moved with sympathy for the "poor Negro." Today the reaction is less of pity for the Negro's condition and more of admiration for the creative genius of the race. This higher evaluation and truer appreciation of the Spirituals are due in a very direct way to the work done by the Harlem group. Paul Robeson and Lawrence Brown, and J. Rosamond Johnson and Taylor Gordon have sung programs made up exclusively of Spirituals before the finest concert audiences in New York and other principal cities of the country. The Hall Johnson Choir has sung with the great orchestras at the Lewisohn Stadium and has appeared in connexion with theatrical productions and on the bills of the big moving-picture theatres. And all of these have broadcast Spirituals. In addition, soloists like Jules Bledsoe, Charlotte Murray, Minnie Brown, and Abbie Mitchell have included these songs in their concert programs. The efforts of these artists have had a far-reaching effect on this new and popular appreciation of the Spirituals. And behind and supplementing the efforts of these and all other artists who have taken the Spirituals to the public has been the work of Harry T. Burleigh and J. Rosamond Johnson in making large numbers of these songs musically available. Because of their work, between two and three hundred Spirituals are in a form that makes them interesting to musical people.

Some creditable work in painting is being done by younger artists, but neither in Harlem nor in the whole country has there been produced in this decade or any other, for that matter, a Negro painter who has achieved anything like the eminence of H. O. Tanner, for some time now dean of American painters in Paris. Aaron Douglas of the Harlem group has won recognition for his black and white drawings. His work has marked originality and has gained for him a place as an illustrator of books. Some creditable work has been done by several students in sculpture, but here, as in painting, the Negro must go back to a former generation for outstanding achievement. But the strangest and most surprising lack is that with all the great native musical endowment the race is conceded to possess, the Negro in New York has not in this most propitious time produced an outstanding composer. The American Negro composers of prominence belong, too, to a former generation.

TWENTY

H ARLEM IS STILL IN THE PROCESS of making. It is still new and
mixed; so mixed that one may get many different views—which
is all right so long as one view is not taken to be the whole picture.
This many-sided aspect, however, makes it one of the most interesting
communities in America. But Harlem is more than a community; it is
a large-scale laboratory experiment in the race problem, and from it a
good many facts have been found.

It has often been stated as axiomatic that if Negroes were
transported to the North in large numbers, the race problem with
all of its acuteness and inflexibility would be transferred with them.
Well, more than two hundred thousand Negroes live in the heart of
Manhattan, nearly a hundred thousand more than live in any Southern
city, and do so without race friction. These two hundred thousand
Negroes have made themselves an integral part of New York citizenry.
They have achieved political independence and without fear vote for
either Republicans, Democrats, Socialists, or Communists. They
are represented in the Board of Aldermen by two members; they are
represented in the State Assembly by two members; they are represented
on the Civil Service Commission by Mr. Ferdinand Q. Morton, and by
two lawyers in the District Attorney's office. They are represented in

the public schools by several hundred teachers; they are represented on the police force by over a hundred men. Recently Dr. Louis T. Wright, a prominent Negro physician of Harlem, was appointed a police surgeon. At the Harlem Hospital, one of the units of the city hospital system and the second largest in Manhattan, one-third of the staff is made up of Negro surgeons and physicians. Four of these are heads of departments, and one, Dr. L. T. Wright, is a member of the Hospital Board and is its secretary. It is true that Harlem is still lacking in many things. Economic development has not kept pace with the development in politics, in the professions, and in the arts. But there has been growth in business, and there is promise that it will increase. There are a number of small concerns, and at present a movement is on foot to establish a system of chain stores. In making comparisons on this point, it must be borne in mind that there is an absence from Harlem of the "Jim Crowism" which in a certain manner works to the advantage of Negro business men in many communities. But in the end this will serve only to make the Negro business man in Harlem a better business man. Harlem was for a number of years the home of Mrs. C. J. Walker, a woman who was an organizer of business on a national scale. She taught the masses of coloured women a secret age-old, but lost to them—the secret every woman ought to know. She taught them the secret of the enhancement of feminine beauty, and on it she built a business that covered not only the United States but also the West Indies. She began life in the most humble circumstances imaginable, but made a fortune and died in her own luxurious home at Irvington-on-Hudson. Notwithstanding, it is idle to expect the Negro in Harlem or anywhere else to build business in general upon a strictly racial foundation or to develop it to any considerable proportions strictly within the limits of the patronage, credit, and financial resources of the race.

Above are cited some of the internal effects of this laboratory experiment. There are also external effects. Forces are going out that are reshaping public sentiment and opinion; forces that are going far towards smashing the stereotype that the Negro is nothing more than a beggar at the gates of the nation, waiting to be thrown the crumbs of civilization. Through his artistic efforts the Negro is smashing this immemorial stereotype faster than he has ever done through any method he has been able to use. He is making it realized that he is the possessor of a wealth of natural endowments and that he has long been a generous giver to America. He is impressing upon the national mind the conviction that he is an active and important force in American life; that he is a creator as well as a creature; that he has given as well as received; that his gifts have been not only obvious and material, but also spiritual and aesthetic; that he is a contributor to the nation's common cultural store; in fine, he is helping to form American civilization.

These forces are helping to bring about an entirely new national conception of the Negro; are placing him in an entirely new light before the American people. Indeed, they placed the Negro in a new light before himself. They have helped to change many of the connotations of the very word "Negro." And these forces are operating not only upon New York and the United States, but upon public sentiment throughout the world.

The Negro in New York still has far, very far yet, to go and many, very many, things yet to gain. He still meets with discriminations and disadvantages. But New York guarantees her Negro citizens the fundamental rights of citizenship and protects them in the exercise of those rights. Possessing the basic rights, the Negro in New York ought to be able to work through the discriminations and disadvantages. His record beginning with the eleven three hundred years ago proves that he can; and he will.

INDEX